Up Here...

A 10th Mountain Soldier's Letters Home
1943 - 1945

10th Mountain Insignia Pin
Vires Montesque Vincimus
"We conquer the greatest mountains"

David T. Hoople

Name: David T. Hoople
Title: Up Here…A 10th Mountain Soldier's Letters Home 1943 - 1945
Cover Design: Linda Spring
Book Design: Margaret G. Hoople

Printed in the United States of America

Cover from Sheet Music for the Song of the 10th Mountain Infantry

Captain

Men of steel and sons of Mars,
Under freedom's stripes and stars
We are ski men
We are free men
And mountains are our home,
Sling your packs and mount your skiis
Stem the slopes thru rocks and trees
Let echos ring with the song we sing
Snap out the cadence with your rifle sling,

Men

Sir! We follow where you go,
Match our foe-men blow for blow
With our mule pack we will bivouac
On freedom's mountain heights,
And from global icy slopes
With our cramp-ons, pick and ropes
Let our B-A-R echo near and far
Loved ones at home will be our guiding star.

Chorus

They call us white clad G.I. Joe
We're the phantoms of the snow,
On our ski boards we're the mountain infantry,
Happy go lucky free
And from Kiska to the Alps
Where the wind howls thru our scalps
With a slap slap slap of a pack against our back
We will bush wack on to victory.

- Song of the Mountain Infantry
Words by W.T. Levitt
Music by Frank Holz

ACKNOWLEDGMENTS

I would like to express my gratitude to my Grandmother, Nelda Rautenberg Hoople, for having the love and foresight to save these letters so that they could be handed down to future generations.

To my sister, Maren Hosmer, I owe decades of thanks for conserving all the letters and pictures related to our family and our father's war experience when the rest of us had no safe place to keep them. She was fiercely protective of them, and then, very generous with them when the time was right. As the youngest sibling, her intense loyalty has been a model of familial love and grace for the rest of us. It has helped bring us back together over the years.

A special thanks to the generosity of Ms. Coi E. Drummond-Gehrig, Digital Image Collection Administrator at the Denver Public Library, for granting permission to use important photographs related to the story this book tells. They are instrumental in illustrating the devastation that Italy suffered during WWII. May they serve as a reminder to future generations of the cruelty of war.

To my good friend, Bill LaCasse, I extend my gratitude for his enthusiasm and encouragement early in the project. He made me feel that this was a worthwhile endeavor when I had doubts that I was up to the task or that anyone would be interested. Thanks, Bill.

To Carolyn Porter, graphic designer and author of her book, "Marcel's Letters", I extend my thanks as she and her book provided me with inspiration while I was bogged down in the middle of this project. After contacting her by email to express my gratitude, she responded with encouragement and positive suggestions. Thank you Carolyn, for your kindness and example of perseverance in your journey.

I would like to thank my cousin, Howard Gordon Hoople, for providing me with genealogical documents on the Rautenberg family that shed light on the family's origin in Germany and their migration to the United States.

I am forever grateful to Joe Caruso, our intrepid guide and translator on our trip to Italy in 2001. His inquisitive and adventurous spirit led us to the village of Tole'. There we made a friend in Davide Demaria and discovered fascinating details pertaining to my father's letters.

To Davide Demaria, I am deeply grateful for the generosity and warm hospitality he extended to us while we were wandering around the Mt. Croce battlefield above Tole' in 2001. I am still in touch with him and he has provided many old and current photographs of great interest to this project.

My thanks to Peter Benoit of Alaska, for generously giving me books and materials from his personal library pertaining to the 10th Mountain Division. His father was also a Mountain trooper in the 10th.

To my wife Maggie, I am eternally indebted for her many, many hours of editing, formatting, and design. Using her professional skills and unlimited patience, she turned my "index finger typed" manuscript into a living and breathing historical document. Her insistence on accuracy and consistency struck a wonderful balance with my limited technological skills and my unlimited "story telling" ability. I cannot thank her enough. I could not have done it without her, just like everything that is meaningful in my life.

"All people are living histories—which is why History matters

...In all cases, understanding History is integral to a good understanding of the condition of being human. That allows people to build, and, as may well be necessary, also to change, upon a secure foundation. Neither of these options can be undertaken well without understanding the context and starting points. All living people live in the here-and-now, but it took a long unfolding history to get everything to NOW. And that history is located in time-space, which holds this cosmos together, and which frames both the past and the present."

©Penelope J. Cornfield, 2008

INTRODUCTION

In 1827 in the Schleswig-Holstein territory of Germany, my great, great grandfather, Adolph Wilhelm Leopold Rautenberg, was born and baptized a Lutheran. He grew up amidst the turmoil of a centuries-old controversy in the region, referred to as "The Schleswig-Holstein Question". Denmark, with its weakened modern monarchy, claimed original ownership of the area to its south, while Germany's nationalism and its growing imperialism proclaimed dominance in this territory to its north.

Both Germans and Danes inhabited this rich farmland. It had desirable coastlines on both the Baltic Sea, to the east and to the North Sea, on the west. Fishing, agriculture, and commerce had been well established economic advantages of the region for centuries. As Western Civilization supposedly matured, many territorial wars continued throughout Europe. Wilhelm Rautenberg, as he was known, attended Michalis Jr. College as a young teen. After three years, he left school and went to work for a merchant, eager to make his way in the world. By 1850, at the age of twenty-three, he decided that military life offered more stability and better pay. There was, after all, the constant threat of war with Denmark, and by then, he had a wife and two children to support. After his military service, he re-established himself as a merchant. After four years of ups and downs, he failed to make ends meet. He ended up in bankruptcy. Frustrated, but full of energy and optimism, he applied for a visa to America on March 30, 1858. He had heard of the opportunities in this young country and he was ready and willing for a new start. The young Rautenberg family arrived in New York sometime later in 1858. Now known as William, he found work in the Empire Woolen Mill in upstate New York. His new country had its own political problems, and soon, the United States was on the verge of civil war. His previous military experience and German heritage made him a prized recruit to help enlist and lead other German-Americans. In 1861, he was commissioned as a 1st lieutenant in the 14th N.Y Volunteer Regiment. They fought in the Seven Days Battle (June 1862), Malvern Hill (July 1862) and Fredericksburg (December 1862).

Sometime in early 1863, Wilhelm and Mathilda had another child. At that time he was probably in the Eastern Theater with the Army of the Potomac. The mission for the Union forces was to provide protection for the Capitol, Washington, D.C., while attempting to defeat the relentless Rebel forces. The Rebel Army seemed to have infiltrated the entire countryside of Maryland and Virginia. They kept the Union forces off balance and the citizenry of Washington, D.C. in constant terror of invasion. The Union army was repeatedly challenged by the aggressive Rebels and their skilled commanders. Also, they were constantly at a disadvantage caused by their indecisive leadership and the toxic mix of military and political aspirations throughout the upper ranks in the field and in Washington. It added up to a stalemate that was costing the Union a staggering number of casualties and much popular disaffection.

Everything that William had pledged and fought for in this new country came down to one thing in his mind—his family was the reason he did all this. He wanted to be with his wife and to see his new baby at this important family moment. He left camp without orders or papers and managed to make it home.

It was a bittersweet reunion as the thirty-six year old lieutenant was soon arrested for desertion. Desertion during the Civil War was punishable by death, usually by a firing squad in front of your fellow soldiers. Thankfully, William's neighbor was the Ohio State Senator John Sherman, brother of Union General William Tecumseh Sherman. Apparently the Senator spent time at a farm in Oneida County, New York, when he was away from his work in Washington D.C. William had probably worked on Sherman's farm at some time and gained the respect of the Senator. The Senator vouched for William back in Washington, and he was not court martialed for desertion. William eventually ended up with his family in Syracuse, New York, where he died in 1877 at the young age of fifty.

Twenty-one years later, a granddaughter of his, Nelda Mathilda Rautenberg, was born to Theodore Herman Rautenberg and Emma Meebold Rautenberg. Theodore Rautenberg was more successful in his business dealings than his father. This Rautenberg generation grew up as middle class Americans living in a fashionable brownstone complete with servants and the first Stanley Steamer automobile in their neighborhood.

Nelda Mathilda Rautenberg, circa 1906

Nelda was a "turn of the century" American girl instilled with proper Late Victorian attitudes and seasoned with strong German family values. When she wrote letters, her prose and cursive script was elegant. She often included a verse of poetry at the close of a letter to enhance the message. Nelda graduated from Syracuse University in 1920. She married Howard Cranford Hoople, and by 1924, had two sons, Howard Jr. and Theodore Gordon. Although the Hooples were of German and Dutch ancestry, both the Hoople sons would interrupt their college years to serve in the U.S. Military during World War II, fighting against German aggression.

Eighty-one years after German immigrant, William Rautenberg, volunteered in the American Civil War to protect and preserve the United States, his great grandson, nineteen-year-old Theodore Hoople volunteered to fight for the preservation of that same Democracy and Liberty but did so on the world theatre. By 1942, the aggressive German Third Reich, under Adolph Hitler, was threatening all of Europe and the free world.

By volunteering, Ted got to choose the branch of service he wanted. The newly formed Mountain Troops attracted his attention and competitive spirit. Ted's military service would take him to the intensive training grounds of Camp Hale, Colorado, high in the Rocky Mountains; to the desert-like terrain of Camp Swift, Texas; and ultimately, to the peaks of the Italian Apennines. He often used the term in his letters, "Up here", so this seemed like the perfect title. Subliminally, it signifies the separate reality, both geographically and mentally, of which he was a part.

His letters and pictures were lovingly saved and cataloged by his mother, Nelda. They were packed away in a small, cloth-upholstered trunk for years. Eventually, I inherited them, but there were so many letters and my grief from losing my Father too early kept me from reading the entire collection. Every time I would delve into them, I could hardly get past a page before I would choke up. I would just put them away and say to myself, "I can't go there right now, maybe someday".

In early April, 2001, I went on a vacation trip to Italy with my wife, Maggie, my sister-in-law, Ellen, and her husband Joe Caruso. Joe's father had emigrated from Italy to the United States right after WWII and had a successful medical practice and wonderful family in Ohio. Joe was an entrepreneur, interested in real estate and traveled often to Italy. He spoke fluent Italian and was a tireless and generous guide. The first two days and nights we stayed in Rome. Joe asked me if there was anything specific I wanted to see in Italy. I told him I always wanted to find Tole' and see where my father was wounded during World War II. This was a time before I Phones and Google Maps, and I had never been able to locate Tole' on a printed map of Italy. I was sure it was a small village, and perhaps it didn't even exist anymore. Joe just nodded his head and said, "We'll see what we can do".

The next day was Good Friday, and we had planned to go to the Vatican expressly to see the Sistine Chapel, among everything else that special day had to offer. While standing in the long, barely-moving lines down the endless halls to the Sistine Chapel, I amused myself with the beautiful, old frescos on the walls. Mostly they were centuries-old maps of the holdings of the Holy Roman Empire during different Papal Reigns. As I tried to orient myself to the different regions being portrayed, there, near the ceiling was a small village marked Tole' with mountains painted around it. That had to be it! It was north/northwest of Florence. Now I had a bearing.

That evening, I bought a large detailed road map of Italy, and we located it on the north slope of the Apennine foothills. It appeared to be about seventy-five miles above Florence, way off the normal tourist routes. It was probably out of our reach, I thought, and we only had two days left on our trip.

We were headed up to Florence on Easter Sunday to take in the city and the pomp and celebration of Easter. We finished up our whirlwind tour of Florence around 2:30 P.M. We had absorbed the beauty of the Cathedral, the Uffizi, Michelangelo's David, Ponte Vecchio and the Palazzo Vecchio. It was a special spring day for us. With our next couple of hours' destination undecided, Joe asked if I would like to try to find Tole'. I said sure, but it was around 2:30 P.M. and Rome was 273 kilometers south. I wasn't sure the girls would be enthusiastic about heading north at this hour. Joe did his best "Pied Piper" imitation and the girls agreed to "go for a ride" into the mountains without any "Quid pro quo". I knew it could be a long way through the mountains to find Tole' and an even longer ride back to Rome that night. What had I gotten myself into? I accepted the fact that, if this didn't work out, there was probably going to be a very expensive dinner, for two couples, in my near future.

We had the imagined route planned out on the map the night before just in case. It looked simple enough. We zoomed out of Florence, headed for the mountains. Joe loved driving the Alfa Romeo rental like he was Mario Andretti. The switchbacks up into the mountains seemed like they would never end. The sage colored hills and granite peaks were glowing in the afternoon April sun. It was a perfect spring day and on we roared, always upwards. Well into the second hour we came upon as "S" curve where the road leveled off. Joe slowed to a stop right next to a small green sign that simply said, Tole'. I got out and took a picture as proof that we had found it. Then what to do?

We proceeded down a hill and cruised on to what appeared to be the main street of a small town. I proposed we stop for refreshments, and I would raise a toast to my father and the men of the 10th Mountain. I got three "Ayes" as we pulled up to the only likely-looking establishment, the Hotel Falco d'Oro. Inside was a typical small hotel bar with a dining area adjacent to it. A local family was quietly dining on the last course of their Easter dinner. I ordered bourbon and in a low and respectful tone saluted the 10th Mountain. The bartender had been brusque, bordering on rude. I supposed we were interrupting a family's quiet Easter dinner and weren't as welcome as we had been in more metropolitan restaurants earlier that week. I decided to go outside and take some photographs of the town and the beautiful surrounding countryside while Joe and the girls finished their refreshments.

After about fifteen minutes, Joe came out looking for me. He asked why I had stepped out so abruptly. I replied that I thought the manager of the inn was rather rude to us, and I was interested in getting some photographs. He laughed and said, "Yeah, he acted a little strange at first, but I had a great conversation with him." Joe shared that the manager thought we were German tourists and, apparently, they are still not fond of Germans around there. He told us that the 10th Mountain troops liberated the town from three years of hell and saved them from the Nazis. The town was still grateful and had recently erected a small memorial chapel on Mt. Croce. "It's just above town up that road where the battle took place. Why don't we take a look?"

It was a short and steep drive up to the top of Mt. Croce, directly above the town. It had a grassy and lightly wooded crest of just a couple of acres, like a lot of the surrounding hill and ridges. These were the northern foothills of the Apennines that led down to the Po Valley. There was the chapel there—a small rendition of the church at the bottom of the hill. We sat at one of the two picnic tables and gazed at the 360 degree view. Hmm, perfect for a German artillery observation post, I thought.

At the other picnic table sat a couple at ease, not looking at all like German tourists. Joe went over and spoke with them in Italian. They were locals. The gentleman offered to show us all that he knew about the battlefield. He was enthusiastic that we were connected to the 10th

Mountain, and said that he had grown up here and knew the local history. With Joe translating, we learned his name was Davide Demaria. He was about my age (50 at that time), and his father had fought far away on the Russian Front, but had made it back, safely, to Tole'. The battle where my Father had fought and been wounded was right in the Demaria's backyard!

As it turned out, Davide had spent his youth rummaging around the hills, collecting memorabilia. He took us down the slope twenty yards and pointed out some depressions in the grass. "Americano, Americano", Joe translated, saying this was where the Americans had dug their shallow foxholes on the morning of April 16, 1945. Thirty yards up over the crest at the edge of the woods were some deeper trenches. "Tedeschi, Tedeschi", Davide pointed out. These were the German dugouts where the artillery observers were probably entrenched with machine guns for protection. I could not believe how close the foxholes and the trenches were to each other. I was convinced we were standing right on the same ground where my father had been wounded on that April morning in 1945.

Davide invited us back to his house just down the hill. It was of a chalet type construction, and we entered through the ground floor into his recreation room. He offered us some wine, and he proceeded to show us the collection of items he had recovered from the battlefield over the years. There was a rusted German machine gun, helmets, grenades, bayonets, ammunition, and all assortments of gear, mostly German. Apparently, they had dropped everything that day, and either fled or got captured. It was then that his wife opened up and told the story of the brutality of the Germans.

When the Germans came and took over her family's farmhouse, her parents had five minutes to gather what cherished possessions they could and get out. Then the Germans proceeded to destroy everything that was left. No wonder the townspeople still hated the Germans. Davide said that it is still such an emotional subject that they don't even mention the occupation or the war in local school history lessons. Then he handed me two tiny amber bottles as a memento of our meeting. They were bottles that held Halazone tablets the G. I.s carried in their battle packs to treat the water in their canteens. He had found those in his days of searching woods and fields for souvenirs. We exchanged addresses and promised to stay in contact. Thanks to Joe's sense of adventure and fluent Italian, we had made new friends while having a once-in-a-lifetime experience. It was at this time in my life that I stopped using the word "coincidence".

We headed back to Rome that evening with the spring sun low in the sky and Joe relishing the Autostrada speed limit of 130 km/h. It had been a remarkable way to end a dazzling six day tour of Italy.

Upon returning home, I wrote Davide a letter in May of 2001. I thanked him for his kindness, hospitality, and for sharing his knowledge of the World War II history of the village that had been in the back of my mind for years. I hoped that we would meet again. I did not hear back from him until I received this letter 18 years later.

Dear Mr David Hoople   25/02/19

My name is Davide Demaria, in 2001 we met in Tolé (Italy), on a mountain called "Monte Croce" unfortunately the letter you sent me, was lost.

I have found it after years but the address is no more legible.
I have found the address in internet, hope you are the person i met.
I would like to send you some pictures, i took in the places your father fought.
Thanks, Hope to hear you soon

Demaria Davide

It was at this point that I knew it was time to get my father's letters back out of storage in order to start the process of reading each and every one of them and of writing what has become this book.

I hope you enjoy my journey as much as I did. I had the joy of getting to know my father better and to experience an unedited display of his sense of humor that was woven through his letters home. I was also able to travel with him through his 10th Mountain journey and experience his transition from a 19-year old enlistee to a full-fledged man, shaped forever through his military experience "up there".

NOTE FROM THE AUTHOR

In the process of transcribing the letters, I randomly made corrections to spelling and grammar thinking it would be easier for the reader. When my editor discovered this, she lobbied to revert back to the original text, citing historical authenticity as the rule of thumb for this type of manuscript. We agreed and spent many hours re-reading the letters and changing everything back to its original form. Remember this was a nineteen-year-old soldier, away from home for the first time, under the stress of rigorous military training and, later, the stress of close combat. Sometimes he was writing in a U.S.O. club or in his barracks late at night, tired and short of time. Sometimes, he was in a tent in sub-zero weather, and overseas, he was often in a foxhole. Later, when he was in the hospitals recuperating, he had to write with his right hand until his left arm healed.

The moniker he signs after many of the closings was most likely a nickname given to him when he was a toddler. The implications are obvious. Why it stuck with him so long is curious but no doubt it helped him to become extremely competitive and tough. The fact that he stops using it, for the most part, after he experiences combat is very telling.

Also, at the suggestion of the editor, we were able to scan the original letterheads and postcards and some of the corresponding letters. The different fonts used for the different letter writers were chosen by the editor and me to reflect the personalities or tone of the letter writers. We also included any sketches that accompanied the letters for authenticity and entertainment. Several of the photographs are from my family's private collection. For those that are not, I have assigned proper credit.

Up Here…
A Tenth Mountain Soldier's Letters Home
1943 – 1945

May 1940 - The American Alpine Club urges the War Department to introduce mountain warfare training to the U.S. Army. By the end of the war the German Army will have fielded 14 mountain divisions, two of which saw combat in Italy.

18 July 1940 - Charles Minot Dole, Chairman of the National Ski Patrol Committee, writes a letter to President Roosevelt, offering to recruit experienced skiers to help train troops in ski patrol work. Citing the effectiveness of ski troops in Finland's defense against the Soviet invasion, Dole points out that "in this country there are 2,000,000 skiers, equipped, intelligent, and able. I contend that it is more reasonable to make soldiers out of skiers than skiers out of soldiers." FDR's reply refers the matter to the War Department for study.

15 November 1941 - Mountain warfare training on a scale larger, then a single patrol begins with the activation of 1st Battalion 87th Mountain Infantry Regiment at Fort Lewis, Washington. Colonel Onslow S. Rolfe creates the first American regiment of mountain troops from scratch.

7 December 1941 - The Japanese attack on Pearl Harbor pushes the U.S. into a war for which it is not ready. Astounded Americans united behind President Roosevelt. Enlistments exceed the capacity of the armed forces to handle them. The barracks at Fort Lewis fill rapidly, and soon the Army is

considering activating another two battalions of the 87th Mountain Infantry.

April 1942 - Construction of Camp Hale begins in the high Rockies near Pando, CO, named in honor of General Irving Hale, who had been chief of the Colorado National Guard.

3 September 1942 - The Mountain Training Center (MTC), with Col. Rolfe in command, is activated at Camp Carson, CO. As the provisional command of a new mountain division, the MTC's mission is to develop procedures and manuals, test equipment and conduct training in mountain warfare.

16 November 1942 - The MTC command moves from Camp Carson to Camp Hale. Currently the MTC command contains only one infantry regiment, the 87th. By the next July, it would include the 86th Infantry Regiment and two artillery battalions along with several special units.

18 November 1942 - 3rd 87th moves from Fort Lewis to Camp Hale.

4-13 February 1943 - Minot Dole visits Camp Hale and sends a report to Washington to Col. Ridgley Gaither that expresses grave concern for the low state of the 87th morale, the inadequacy of tactical training, and the high daily sick rate, including many cases of the "Pando Hack" caused by breathing smoke produced by coal burning furnaces and trains. (The 9200' elevation combined with cold air temperatures caused almost all the smoke produced to be pushed down and hang over the valley for days at a time.)

March 1943 - Ted leaves his freshman studies at Syracuse University and enlists in the Army hoping to join the 10th

Mountain Division. It is a widely publicized and intriguing new unit in the Army, seeking skiers, mountaineers, and other adventurous, athletic, young men. This would be right up his alley and provide him with many meaningful connections later in civilian life to other veterans of the 10th.

INDUCTION, FORT DEVENS, MA

Ted Hoople as a 19-year old Army inductee

Note to Ted from cousin Sally:

March 9, 1943

Dear Ted,

Don't forget to request the branch of Service you want when you get to the Induction Station. And don't forget to use this this car ticket, it will save you .10 cents.

As always,

Sally

Letter to Ted from Grandmother Rautenberg:

March, 10 1943

My Dear Teddy,

I hope by now you are comfortably tucked in your barracks and have waited to open my letter as I have asked you to. Eighteen years young and Uncle Sam has called you to the Colors for which I am very proud, I hope you are comfortable tucked into your first sleeping quarters in your first night in the Army, and have experienced a thrilling first day. As you travel along, your mind and your physical being will expand and you will experience many happy hours along with some unpleasant ones.

Make the best of all your opportunities, seek out the best crowd, and travel with them. With the background and training you've had, I shall not worry about you, for I believe you will live up to our trust in you.

Enclosed is Pop's pocket Testament—I did not think to ask him if I could let you take it along. He thinks a great deal of it, and he would want it to travel with you. I am sure you will regard it as one of your most precious possessions.

Author's Note: *The rest of this letter from Grandmother Rautenburg is missing as is the Pocket Testament which he kept in his left breast pocket at all times including and through combat. It would later serve as a disturbing piece of memorabilia. The upper right corner was burned off as a result of the red-hot shrapnel that passed within inches of his heart and wounded him in his upper left arm two years later.*

Ted's postcard to his parents from Fort Devens Ayer, MA

March 12, 1943

Dear Folks,

First chance I've had to sit down. Been going through the mill the last 2 days. Started out Wed. at 8 AM, inducted, sent out here (Fort Devens), classified etc. went to bed 12:30 AM, got up at 4:30. I'm pooped. I need a shave, a haircut, and a shower. Get it when I have time. I met lots of Belmont kids and Syracuse fellows (Doug S.). Write a letter when I get shipped.

Love,

Ted

P.S. Don't send mail

Ted's postcard to Gram from Chicago, IL

Mar 16, 1943

Dear Gram,

   Enjoying a wonderful trip. Have 10 hrs. free here in Chicago. Can't find where Elzea (ha ha) lives or I would certainly call. I'm disappointed!! Travelling first class pullman; all on the gov't.

   USO here has treated me wonderful. Free shows etc. Too bad I can't see Aunt Mary either, makes me mad. Well, love anyway,

Ted

March 16, 1943

Dear Mother,

Traveling with 6 other Mtn. Troopers. Left March 15. Enjoyed a long stay here in Chicago. Trying still to phone your sweet cousin, (no luck as yet). Having neat time in Pullman reservations. Leaving now on the Santa Fe for Colorado.

Love,

Ted

P.S. Tried to call you Sunday afternoon!!

March 18, 1943
(from Pueblo, CO)

Dear Mother,

I've had the most wonderful trip so far. I'm now writing from Pueblo, Col. where I have five hours layover before I catch the next train to Pando.

While I was in Chicago, I tried my best to locate your dear sweet cousin, but I couldn't, but I will on a return trip, if I can obtain his address.

East of Chicago the change in the type of land was only slight in that it was more level than New England, but west of Chicago I found the land was very flat and barren, especially in Missouri and Kansas. In Kansas I got my first view of the oil fields, which extended as far as you could see across the flat land. I also saw lots of tumbleweeds racing across the fields; it moves very fast.

The last train exchange will be the prettiest so I am informed, so I'll close here as I am about ready to leave.
Much Love,
Ted
P.S. I've had many wonderful hours spent in the U.S.O.s. The Clubs in Chicago impressed me most, for there everything is free, even a photograph which will be sent to you and Betty (please inform her).
P.S. Sorry I picked up such a poor pen

TRAINING, CAMP HALE, CO

March 29, 1943

Dear Gram,

Here I am and what a place 10,000 ft. in the air. I feel great and as everyone else puts it, "Never felt better in my life". Here's the situation; my barracks is in quarantine for two weeks. In other words, I won't be able to get out, probably until April 7th!

If you should come through Grand Junction, the train definitely stops at Pando, which I can reach very easily, but it would be inadvisable to stay at our guest house because it is about two miles from the railroad and I don't think there is any means of transportation.

I sure hope that everything works out so that I can see you again before we ship out. Please excuse such briefness but time is the only element.

Love,

Teddy

March 30, 1943

Hello Mom,

How's the gal? I feel swell- cold completely heeld. I wrote Gram immediately but I have little hope of seeing her because our Company is in quarantine for two weeks. Never the less, I wrote her the details cause Bill (Hoople, first cousin also 10th MTN) told me what to do.

We are fully equipped now except for our skis, darn it. We have swell rucksacks like we used at Camp Beckett only much better. We are in intensive training now since we have a full company.

Do you know what would please me the most? A nice box of cookies, candy, gum, my sweat socks, and a cheap time keeper (that's because up here we are designated to be at certain places at certain times and if we are not there-OH OH! And I have to depend upon my friends for the time). I think that I won't need to spend any money. All I have to do is write home for everything I need. That reminds me, I need as many coat hangers as possible, they don't even sell them up here and we've just got to have them.

Army life is a snap. There is absolutely no better training for the service than summer camps. Honestly, I'm so far advanced in taking care of my bunk and clothes that it seems much nicer than I had anticipated.

There's still plenty of snow on the slopes for skiing but down here it's melting very fast. My uniform is getting woefully dirty and that's going to be a pretty cleaning bill. By George, it just started snowing again. This branch of the service requires twice as much clothing and equipment. Why I have two big duffle bags full of stuff now. It's awful easy to lose stuff but I have already bought some indelible ink and tagged everything, including my shoes.

One thing surprised me when I took my Physical, one of my eyes is a little off which gave me poor eyesight as a physical defect. They were 20/20 and 20/30. That's the first I ever knew of that.

Tell Betty to write cause I've received only two letters and I'm "going over the mountain" if she doesn't write. I received two tiny postcards from Totsie, (Brother Howard). He's a shrewd apple.

I am looking forward to seeing a woman pretty soon. This is absolutely the longest I have ever gone. Wow! I'm a wild man Woo woo! Sometime in the next six months, if we're still around, I'll have a 14 day furlough like Bill is getting very soon. I would like to spend a few hours in Chicago seeing the relatives so sometime give me their addresses.

I must write to my second love now. Good-bye.

Love,

Teddy

April 5, 1943

Dear Pop,

You addressed your letter to the wrong Company, and it finally ended up with Bill, who brought it down. I am in the 86th; you addressed it to the 87th (Author's note: Ted was later transferred to the 87th). Thanks a lot. It has been a long necessity.

As you know, our company has been in quarantine for two weeks, but tonight we were allowed privileges and so some of us went to the Post Exchange and then to a show. Two weeks is a darn long time when you count the minutes.

We're really going through the ropes fast. We've had an awful lot of lectures and field work. You cannot imagine what a break I got through camping. Why I'm so far ahead of most of the fellows just from camp training. The little things I got from camping like knowing how to make a bed (you'd be surprised how stupid some fellows are) or timing yourself with regularity of a day's program. In short, I enjoy it. It's a man's life, especially up here.

Sunday, our CO (commanding officer) asked for fellows who wanted to climb one of these surrounding hills. Anybody who says our officers are pussy footers is full of baloney. He kept us going at a terrific pace. He's from V.M.I. and as rugged as they make'em.

So far, we have not started skiing but from all sources we are supposed to start next week. It was terrifically cold when I first arrived, at least zero several days, but now the sun has gone to work and melted all the snow in the camp area. The air is so thin and free of dust that when the sun comes out it makes it very easy to get a sunburn. Although the snow has left here there will be skiing until later June on the higher slopes where we'll train.

We have a German kid in our Squad. He made an escape from Germany in 1938 with his parents. His father was a professor of Fine Arts at Homburg. His father's name is on the Black List now. His description of the escape was a photo finish. They just got across the border when the Gestapo arrived at the border. The only thing the Gestapo could do was shoot, darn lucky they missed.

I've certainly got some beautiful equipment. Up here we've got at least twice as many outfits as any other Branch receives. We have a uniform for every occasion and footwear too.

I'll cut off here. Thanks for sending the money order. Like you said, there are a million things you got to get, it's a problem. I seem to be the longest letter writer around, even Betty (please quote to her if you get a chance) doesn't go beyond the first page.

Tell Mom I won't love her unless she sends my order. Don't forget some cookies, etc.

Yours,

Ted

April 9, 1943

Dear Mom,

I received your letter today. Air Mail will arrive here two days sooner, which would help plenty. If you want me to write you Air Mail, why I'd be glad if you send me some stamps. I'm sorry about the stale news, Betty complains of that also, but I too receive stale mail. Let's compromise and write Air Mail.

I'm going to have a picture taken of me in my white uniform. When that comes you must promise to burn up that one from Chicago.

This is a beautiful day because yesterday we had a blizzard. The mountains look beautiful in the early morning. I received the money order but haven't had a chance to cash it yet since the Post Office closes early and I'm about three quarters of a mile from it.

I got a letter from Totsie today and he didn't like the picture either. He's enjoying himself as far as I can make out. All the parties he's been to with women—Wow. I haven't seen one for three and a half weeks. I see Bill only occasionally—you see quarantine has kept us nicely confined except for training. I'll be expecting a big package from you. All the fellows around here have all sorts of things from home. What have you been doing? Remember what I said, I wanted you to send me stuff often, after all I'm only 35 miles from the nearest town, which has a population of about 5,000. You can buy things here but the supply is not sorted and is very limited.

The reason why I'm able to write now, 3:30 P.M., is that I'm on a special duty. I'm in charge of Headquarters for Company A, (General Pratt). Me and the sergeant are having a chummy time. The afternoon is slow because the Company is out on a hike so I don't have any errands to run.

I've written once a week like you told me. If you had told me more, like Betty did, then you would have gotten more. I've written on the average two letters a day, mostly three, I think. I've written all the guys in Belmont, Grammas twice, Totsie, Betty, and of course you and by George it's tough to keep up on your correspondence but plan a certain time each night to write, so it isn't so hard. You ought to see me with holy socks and smelly feet. Gee, Mom it's a shame all of your good cooking and baking is going to waste. My, what wouldn't I do with one of your chocolate cakes? I guess I'll have to mooch on other fellows who get things from home (Ha-Ha-Hump). The Sargent told me that this is going to be the toughest outfit in the world. Most of the fellows misuse the title and call it the Ski Troops. Well that's just its social name. He said we will start climbing mts. In several months from now. We'll be able to fight anywhere except on the ocean and air. Last summer the 87th almost got shipped to Guadalcanal but the Marines did such a good job that they didn't send them, so says our Commanding General to the Sgt. We will be lugging from 60-90 pound packs all the time and climbing ledges and cliffs. This is going to be great. Boy will we be rugged (ha-ha). The commandos, they're a bunch of sissies. They fight and then they're off for a couple of weeks but us MOUNTAIN BOYS CONTINUALLY GO. Besides looking out for our lives from enemy fire, we've got to have steady nerves for climbing and scaling peaks, etc. Yes, even the fellows I'm with don't realize all their interest is in the direction of skiing.

Good afternoon dear.

Love,
Teddy

Ted (on left) on KP Duty, reprinted from the 10th's Regimental Magazine

April 12, 1943

Dear Ma—

It's 12 P.M. I just got through K.P. Man did we work. I cleaned out a grease trap. If you don't think it's filthy and slimy why just try it. When I got back to my bunk, why I found a package there. Right now I'm in the latrine munching away on some popcorn. I've only a few minutes left to drop a line to "Jonnie" (girlfriend, Betty Johnson).

Thanks that's the best news from home yet. Don't stop now, keep it coming. I get awfully hungry at night. Speaking of night, I must close. Good night.

Love,

Tink

P.S. I got the money order but it also went to Bill H. in the 87th. Poor guy is getting discouraged. I'm too tired to do anything about writing, you figure it out.

15 April, 1943

Dear "Nelly dear",

How's the gal? We went for a lovely run today, about 2 miles and half of a way through a brook. I was complimented by a lieutenant for having the wettest uniform. All the officers ran in it with us. It was fun 'cause I didn't have to worry about going home and catching "H".

One thing that disturbs me, I'm acquiring a bad vocabulary. It's impossible to prevent it. Even the officers give us a good joke once in a while. The "Top Kick" is the worst cusser of them all. Too bad I didn't get a good start while I was home so I could keep up with them (ha-ha). But one thing, this is a man's life in more ways than just that.

I met this guy, Hurlburt. I think he's a drip. I'm sorry, but that's my impression. He's in my company and I met him in the mess hall. He's never heard of "Hoople", so after an exchange of words I dropped the conversation.

Thanks for the socks and coat hangers. They certainly were stuck up at the 87th for a long time. I got them, that's what counts. How about 10 lbs. of fudge or as much as possible. It would cut down my expenses a lot.

Tomorrow I've got a long hike ahead. We've been wearing "bocker" boots and thick socks and do my feet and everyone else's stink. Wow! I hope we can wear our G.I. shoes. Those boots are tough except in the snow. It gets extremely hot when the sun shines but further up the mountains there is plenty of snow for a while. I'm going out skiing Saturday afternoon and try myself out. Our ski instructors will follow soon, I hope.

Guess what Ma? I signed the payroll slip. I'll call you the 1st of May, Betty also. You two arrange it so that I can talk to both of you in one call, because two would cost too much and it takes a day to get a call through. Maybe it will be the second if I can't get it through. Just fifteen days. I can hardly wait.

So far I haven't gone out on a pass. It costs all the fellows that went at least 30 bucks apiece, but most of them booze it up.

I am going to the show to see "Cabin in the Sky" with Duke Ellington and his orchestra. Goodnight Mother, be a good girl. I love you very much (sounds like I'm writing to Betty).

CAMP HALE, *COLORADO*

April 16, 1943

Dear Mom,

I thought you were headed for Syracuse on the 10th. I mailed one about two or three days ago to Syracuse.

Thanks for the watch. It will serve the purpose. I don't see any reason for getting a good watch while I'm taking basic training.

We took a ten-mile hike yesterday into some pretty country. I'll bet there's some wonderful fishing up here. I'll call you at Syracuse on either the 1st or 2nd of May.

Tonight I go on guard duty. I've got to study ten general orders before I go on. I start at 5 P.M. and will be relieved once in a while through the night.

I've got to get some rest so I won't fall asleep on duty. The watch comes in handy here.

I wanted the picture, which was framed. The big one. Gee Whiz, that's the only one I've got that you could call a picture.

Got to take a snooze.

Love,

Ted

P.S. Could I possibly have a little more dough? I'll pay you back, no fooling.

April 1943 (Date and first page missing from Ted's letter to his mother)

...to write Auntie Babe, Cousin Elzie, Nelda Louise, Gram, Totsie, Mrs. A.P. Johnson, and Betty, and a dozen more.

We've been on the firing range and I've qualified as a sharpshooter, only three points from expert. We get up at 5 A.M. fire at 6 and get off the range at 7. Besides cleaning my rifle and doing clean up in the barracks, I'm on the basketball team. We are now in the finals for the 86th regiment championship.

Can you understand why I'm scribbling now? I'm awful tired, Mom. After basic I'll have plenty of time (they say). Goodnight Mother Dear. Next to you comes Betty, but you're still first.

Love,

Tink

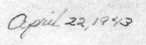

CAMP HALE, COLORADO

April 22, 1943

Dear Gram,

Wow! Were those homemade cookies? All the fellows enjoyed them immensely. They lasted one good night. Most everyone here gets packages and distributes them to all. I never believed the Army had such generous guys.

I went skiing Sunday. It was perfect for a beginner like me. When I fell, I landed up to my hips. Once I had to grab a tree and ... *(Rest of letter missing)*

May 6, 1943

Dearest Mother,

I'm doing my best to get this to you on Mothers' Day. I went on a pass and spent plenty of dough. A hat, fishing equipment, traveling bag, toilet articles, gun cleaning outfit—well at least 30 dollars on necessities. I got 56 bucks pay. Take two phone calls, money for a pass (food, lodging, and traveling).

Your brownies were really delicious. I don't think you ever made any better ones. The fellows were enjoying them too. Gee they were good. I ate them too fast though.

Gram R sent me plenty of things, Gum, cookies etc., everyone writes so much!! I have at least 9 letters ... (Rest of letter missing)

CAMP HALE, COLORADO

May 24, 1943

Dear Mother,

I have a funny feeling that you are all upset about my correspondence. Don't think for a minute that I have forgotten anyone. My only explanation is that I haven't had time, believe me. It is true that I write Betty quite often but it amounts to very little most of the time. I had already written Auntie Babe and both Grams and Totsie.

I did all my laundry this weekend. 6 Pairs of socks, 3 pairs of underwear, 2 fatigue uniforms, leggings, mountain coats, three towels, two sweaters and a half dozen handkerchiefs. I did not have one night free last week. We went on night problems and demonstrations and bivouacs (overnight). In one of the demonstrations several incidents occurred which will amuse you. In this one particular happening, several trees were blown up and holes blasted out of the ground. We were told to watch for flying material (of course we had our helmets on). One rock struck a fellow and shattered his wrist. Another clonked a fellow nearby, right square on his tin helmet. It made a dent big enough for a baseball to rest in. Well he just collapsed to the ground cold as a whistle. He recovered fast and it didn't bother after a few days.

Today we went on another all-day trip up the mountains. Our course was to acquaint ourselves with the fighting defensive lines in the mountains. We also were spending a pleasant afternoon digging fox holes.

I met one kid from Belmont here. I never knew him very well but I knew the girl he was hitching to quite well.

Don't feed Betty any more propaganda about my past. I know darn well by the way she writes that you're talking and a little over doing 'cause she's quite upset 'cause I never told her about my past. She keeps asking me questions about certain people and stuff like that. Loose talk may sink my ship.

I was a bad boy last week and forgot to shave. My goodness, how did I forget? I sure picked a lot of rocks for just one shave.

I've got to drop a line to Nellie Louise also. So, take care of yourself and don't get into any more trouble ha! Ha! Much Love from Tink

P.S. I might call you up next pay day.
P.P.S. I'll send 15 bucks home to save for furlough June 2nd. Please send that picture, I need it very bad.

June 14, 1943

Dearest Mother,

This is an appropriate time to send you this. You know I wouldn't forget your birthday even though it will arrive a little late.

I shall now proceed to dope you up on the news. This weekend I went on a trip with two other fellows. We started Friday night and got back late Sunday. The first night we only got as far as the first mountain, which is 2,000 feet higher than our present location. We made camp about ten P.M. with the assistance of a bright half-moon. We cut boughs of balsam, which made for a comfortable sleep. Our breakfast, at 6:30A.M., consisted of boiled eggs, toast, and cheese dreams, supplied to us by the Mess Sargent before we left. We traveled all day over the mountains, with our destination being Leadville, a small mining town about 15 miles from Camp Hale. During the day it rained and snowed, off and on, but we traveled in comfort as we brought our ski parkas along with us. We arrived at the highest incorporated town in the world, 10,200'. Boy it is a wild place!! Well we ended our excursion by taking the bus back the next afternoon and who should we meet on it but Bill coming back from his furlough AWOL one day. He missed train connections at Chicago.

Now here's some inside news which is not so pleasant to write. Bill's Company (1 87th), while he was on furlough, was out firing mortar shells. There are 4 platoons in each company and one is the Weapons Platoon. A mortar is considered a heavy weapon. Two fellows were firing a shell, not knowing that it was defective, they fired as usual. Tragedy followed. The shell blew up three feet from the ground killing the two soldiers who were firing. They were supposed to go on furlough with Bill but only ten were allowed passes, leaving those two out. I will not describe the mess that followed the explosion, I'll leave that to your imagination. Bill is leaving tomorrow or the next day to catch up with his regiment, which is now in California, destination unknown although they might be on maneuvers.

Oh yes, I almost forgot. I took my fishing equipment on the trip but in my haste, I forgot my reel and line. The opportunities were superb. Darn the luck!!

10th Mountain insignia pin

I hope you like the pin. Betty said that's what you wanted. I had to send to Denver for it which accounts for the delay.

Good night and until I hear from you again,

Lots of Love,

"Tink"

June 2, 1943

CAMP HALE, COLORADO

Dear Gram,

June 21, 1943

Dear Gram, (Hoople)

I guess you have been wondering what has become of me. Frankly, I don't know myself but I do know those dates and nuts were really wonderful. Do you realize how much energy builder was stored in those sweets? After a hard day I'd eat a couple and feel a lot more steady and refreshed after a while.

Well the other day Bill shipped out to the Pacific coast somewhere. He'll probably be stationed there for several weeks or more before leaving. I said goodbye. We had a swell chat about Cranberry Lake and the hut we built up on the hill. I also got some good addresses of neighboring ladies.

I believe, by the look of things that we'll be around here until Jan. 8th anyway. That is not definite of course, but that will be the completion of our mountain training. If they need men in a hurry, though, we are liable to go any time.

Are you planning to go to the Lake at all this summer? I hope you can make it. I know if I had the chance or the dough, etc. I wouldn't miss it for anything. I've got another big day ahead of me tomorrow. We're taking a trip to Homestake Mountain, 13,500 ft. and about 16 miles to the south.

Thanks for the dates. I really appreciate those little packages very much. So far Mom hasn't sent much in that line and I wish she would hop on the ball and send something like that. But all she does is send her love and I guess that ought to satisfy me.

Love, Pvt. Teddy

Dear Mom,

I'm writing right now with my new pencil. It's a peach-
thank you. The cake arrived in good shape but I wasn't
able to read what was on the frosting.

The fellows all had a piece and wanted more. It went
down faster than any torpedoed tanker ever did.

I'm in the process of writing to the bank. I realize that
it should be attended to immediately but as usual it
slipped my mind for a while. I must also write to Mr.
Bennet as he has sent "The Messenger" to me regularly.

I am planning on going to Glenwood Springs on my
birthday. It will cost a lot of money but I'll send the
remains when I get back. Even though a pass costs a lot
of money here, just getting out of Army routine makes
me feel happy and ready when I get back. Seeing that it
is my birthday, I'll use that as an excuse for being so
spend thrifty.

Aunt Mary (Rautenberg) sent me some money as did both
Grams.

Last night I was on guard duty. My reliefs lasted from
6-8 P.M. and 12-2 A.M. I had to challenge all the
soldiers coming in from pass. It was a lot of fun knowing
that you are in charge of a certain area and no one,
including an officer, could pass without your permission.

I'm going on another two-day bivouac tomorrow so I must close now.

Lots of Love,

Tink

P.S. Dear Mrs. Hoople, The cake was very nice. I guess I ate more than Ted did. We sure do go for cake like that.

Sincerely, Ted's bunkmate, Pvt. S. Tilton

(Mom don't believe him–I hid the rest under my bed)

Tink

15 July 1943 - The 10th Light Division (Alpine) with Brigadier General Lloyd E. Jones in command is activated at Camp Hale, thus replacing the MTC. Jones had previously commanded a task force that occupied Cold Bay and Amchitka in the Aleutians.

CAMP HALE
COLORADO

July 15, 1943

Dear Mom,

As to any knowledge of a furlough I'm unaware. I'll drop Aunt Dorothy (Hoople) a card tonight. Please send me your camera with some film so I can take some pictures for you and Betty. I lost Betty's ring today. Tough Luck Kid. I was out on the BAR (Browning automatic rifle) range and somehow it got away from me. I remember having it up until 5 o'clock tonight, so that limits the space. I'm quite sure I'll find it.

Did I tell you Mrs. Johnson sent me a birthday cake exactly like yours along with a box of Schraff's candies? I can't think of any more personal news than that.

Please, if possible, send the camera. I'll keep it for a week and send it right back.

Tilton, my friend who wrote you that P.S. on one of my letters, is from N.H. He's just out of high school. There are at least ten guys from Harvard here that I know pretty

47

well and as many from Yale. Do you know Judge Moutague, his son and I are great pals. Also have you heard of Harry Wareham? Jack McClusky and a bunch of others from Syracuse University.

I'm going on a fishing trip this weekend with Bill Hamilton, the best guy in the Company. He is from Oregon State University, and Bill Kohn from Pennsylvania, the third member of the party.

Did I tell you the camp is being made over to the 10th Alpine Division and at least 100 fellows from the Company are being transferred to the 85th or the 97th, both new regiments? It might mean a break if I get transferred although I'm satisfied right here. I'm running short on time again.

Love,

"Tink"

July 19, 1943

Dear Folks,

I spent a swell weekend up in the mountains with Bill Kohn, the "Pennsylvania Dutchman". We were up about 13,500 feet in the Homestake Mountain area. All along the way we fished and caught some beauties. I found a fly that really lures the fish. It is called the Rio Grande Special. It's nothing more than an oversized mosquito with a couple of wings attached. It took me all day to

48

reach the base of Homestake and when we got there we decided to fish and start right back. There were no Brook Trout in this mountain pond, only Steelheads. They put up quite a fight but they're not as nice as the Brookies. The mountain rises directly above the pond. It's a sheer mass of rock and snow. In crevices the snow could be well over 20 feet.

The enclosed picture was taken after a hard day in the field. As you can see, I'm headed for the shower. I found the ring just where I left it on the firing range. We're still working the range but tomorrow we're off on a three-day bivouac with the Company.

Ted ready to hit the shower

There is a lull before the storm. Transfers are at a temporary standstill until the new organization is regimented. As soon as anything happens I'll let you know.

Betty and I are hitting on only 3 plugs now.

Love,

Ted

July 20, 1943

Dear Pop,

Nelda is sure a hard woman!! Sounds like she is throwing a little harshness in her letters. I guess my problems are lighter than they appear in writing (this pen is going on the blink).

Yesterday we went on a supposedly three-day trip covering 18 miles but two of the three days were to be spent on tactical maneuvers. As you know I've been going to BAR school for two and a half weeks now and we have not completed our firing for record yet. Nevertheless the BAR teams went along. It was only 7 P.M. after our fox holes were dug and tents pitched that they informed the BAR men that they must pack up and leave. The rain made the whole situation complete. We started down the mountain and just as we reached the road I remembered that ring. I had taken it off and hung it on a limb in order to not scratch it while digging my foxhole. As you know, always when traveling alone, there must be three in a party. "Tilt", the cake eater and Hamilton, from Oregon stayed with me while I went back for it. That thing has caused me more trouble than the woman herself. By the time I got back on the road again it was dark. One of our friends, who drives a jeep, picked us up halfway down the mountain. We each had a turn at the wheel which consoled our dispirited minds. We arrived back at the barracks at 11 P.M. and were anxious to catch a good night's rest. But as luck goes, the General was supposed to inspect our barracks the following day and therefore we arose at 4:30 A.M. to clean up before we left for the field.

Today made up for it, though. The only thing we did all day was to operate targets while other BAR teams fired. Lights are about to go out.

As ever,

Ted

29 July 1943 - ATF-9, including the 87th Mountain Infantry, embarks from San Francisco and sails for Adak in the Aleutians to prepare for the invasion of Kiska, which is occupied by Japanese forces. Ted is still assigned to the 85th which is not combat ready yet.

August 2, 1943

Dear Nellie,

Well I came pretty close to 30 didn't I? Perhaps you can bum 2 bucks off Pop to make it an even 30.

How do you like my new address? Pvt. Hoople 31302591, 90th Mt. Inf. 10th Light Div., Camp Hale Colorado. Holy catfish, this Army gets me, why in the heck do they pick a healthy guy like me to work on Supply? I did pretty darn good on the rifle, also. If I don't get a furlough by Sept., which I doubt now, I think the best thing for me to do is try for the paratroops 'cause I won't stand this chicken stuff without even getting a furlough.

A cadre from Hawaii came in and everyone has a ribbon and a few stripes. They're all good guys as they've all been in over 2 years and they know all there is to know about the Army.

Thanks for the cookies. I downed them in about three minutes.

Love from a mad soldier,

Ted

Dear Pop,

Did you by chance meet with Mr. Austin from Reading? I believe he has a son in the junior or senior camp. I ask this because Dick Austin mentioned that he had a younger brother up there. He was in the old Company with me last March and he also got transferred to the 90th with me. He and I are both working in Supply together. He was at Norwich three years and knows more about the army than any of those non-coms. He has the dirtiest deal of anyone. He should be an officer, by rights, but that's the Army for you. He is also trying to get out of S-4 Supply. I think we are getting transferred to a line company pretty soon. All day long I "goldbrick" not because I am one, but there's nothing to do. The Major gave us our OK on the transfer and I will be glad to get a pack on my back. We were practically promised a T rating either at corporal or sergeant, but T ratings are goldbrick ratings in the eyes of regular line men.

I'm working out down at the fieldhouse playing basketball every night. I feel as though I'm getting a better eye, especially set shots. Maybe it's the altitude? I'm also able to run with more endurance and it sure takes a long time to develop it up here. A hundred-yard dash is almost as tiring as a half mile run.

I just had a Wisdom tooth pulled yesterday and the darn thing is still dripping. Another tooth that I won't have to worry about.

I think I have a date this weekend with a girl from Colorado U. I'm kind of lost for funds but that doesn't bother me. I understand she has plenty herself. Sometimes I get the urge to go out and raise ---- with the boys. I don't know why or what satisfaction I'd get from it, but I still have that feeling.

With these furloughs held up I'll go nuts. The Colonel was on a troop ship that got sunk and he's in a big hurry to get out of here, but I understand the new T.O. says next spring we'll be ready.

Got a letter from Gram Hoople saying that I forgot to write her a thank you note. Ahh, me!!

I also met a guy who knows Gillen in Methuen N.J. In fact he lives a mile from him. From what I hear it's really some ritzy burg.

Got to hit the hay for a while,

Ted

11 August 1943 - Troops of the 87th Mountain Division land on Kiska but the Japanese have abandoned the island. One American drowns while engaged in the beach head landing, the first of many 10th Mountain soldiers to die in the line of duty during WWII.

CAMP HALE, COLORADO

August 24, 1943

Dear Mrs. Hoople,

So Pop is going to Herman, that's swell but I sure would like to see him. If you go with him, who's going to be home. I wanted so much to be back again in Belmont but if the job goes first that's just T.S. I'll go there anyways for 4 or 5 days at least. I would like to stop in Chicago but I'm afraid I'd be too anxious to get the train east. I would also like to stop in Syracuse but I'd rather keep right on going just to see you.

Perhaps you haven't heard I'm not the type that boasts but I've a $10,000 insurance policy plus a war bond. My grand total of money for each month amounts to $37 and you still insist I don't send enough home. When you live up here for six months and don't even see a store, you're not going to send a good time home. I can see you still (Betty also) don't realize what kind of place this is. I'm not saying there's anything wrong at all but a guy is bound to get lonesome for a city. Oh well, skip it. Take for instance a camp, any other camp in the country in fact, there are none so isolated as this. It cost at least 15-20 bucks for one pass. The nearest towns are Denver, 170 miles, Grand Junction, 189 miles, Glenwood Springs, 95 miles. All the fellows up here haven't even bothered to send money home. Well I'm not kicking about that so much, but it's your attitude. I wouldn't have said anything about it until you mentioned about the $50 and how much I should save and how much I should take out for war bonds etc.

Boy, when I get home no one is going to tell me where to go and what to do. I've had six months of it and it's time for a break.

I hope you understand my explosion but all I needed was a letter like that one. After all. Nelda. I'm not your little kid anymore. I received your cookies, Mom. I eat 'em just before I go to bed, you know, like I used to sneak into the ice box. Thank Mrs. Sutherland for the kisses. I really appreciate those things a lot.

Another outfit from here shipped out today. For certain reasons I can't tell you who. I've been doing a lot of athletics, lately, basketball especially. I find that most of the fun I get comes from doing sports.

Haven't heard from the Grandmas or Totsie in a long time. Be home soon (in a month or so).

Love,

Tink

23 August 1943 - 10th RECON establishes a rock-climbing school for the 10th Mountain Division at Homestake Creek above Camp Hale.

3 September 1943 - The Allied invasion of Italy begins when British and Canadian troops cross the Straits of Messina and land on the "toe of the Italian boot".

September 3, 1943

Dear Gram (Rautenburg),

Where has your correspondence been? I haven't received an answer from my last letter I sent you.

I almost had a furlough August 15th but I decided I had better wait, thinking, of course, of the complications involving travel to all sorts of places. I should have taken the offer, for now the furloughs have been cancelled indefinitely. I plan to stop off and see you and Gram Hoople and the rest of the clan, on my way to Boston (when I finally get one). I have finally succeeded in transferring to a rifle company again. My new address is as follows: Pvt. T.G. Hoople 31302591, Company I 90th Mt. Inf., A.P.O. 345, Camp Hale Colorado.

Where have you been lately? I haven't heard from you in a long time.

You can't imagine what a help those rags have been in dusting my bed and shelves, cleaning my rifle and lots of other items.

Is Totsie still fussy about things, women, or is he studying very hard?

I heard from unreliable sources that Bill Hoople was in on the raid at Kiska. Luckily there weren't any Japs there. Well, I'm expecting a letter from you real soon.
Love,
Ted

9 September 1943 - Four infantry divisions of the 5th Army force a landing at Salerno, Italy south of Rome. The Italian Army has given up, but Hitler rushes reinforcements to create a defensive line across Italy, massing German artillery and troops. This line of defense is initially named the Winter Line. As the allies advance northward, it becomes reorganized by the Germans as the Gustav line to hold Rome.

September 13, 1943

Dearest Mother,

I was stunned by the last letter from home. I just could not believe it. I hope Gram (Hoople) is OK. It must be very hard for her.

I'm sitting beside the campfire thinking of all the things which have happened while I've been away. I confess, I'm really homesick right now, but when I'm going through training I don't have time to let my mind wander. I'm very conservative with compliments but I will say one thing. You're the best Mother in the whole world and I hope that someday I'll have a wife just like you. Tell me, did you ever jilt a guy before you married Pop? I thought I knew everything about women but I just found out that I haven't begun to know.

How is Pop? I guess it hit him pretty hard too. If you could have informed The Red Cross early enough, I could have been home with the whole family on an emergency furlough.

I hope they open the furloughs up again pretty soon. I can hardly wait to see you and the boys.

The fire is burning with a dull glimmer, which makes it very hard to write, so I'll close now.

With Lots of Love,

Tink

Dear Pop,

You can imagine what a surprise I received in Totsie's letter of a few weeks ago. Everything seemed to be running smoothly and then bingo. You're right, he was everyone's friend and an Uncle whom I've always looked up to and admired. Things like that happen so fast that it is hard to believe, but life can be hard sometimes.

I'm very interested in your coaching. I would like to hear how you make out. Sure it's OK. I'm glad to see the socks can be of some use. Give me the dope on the formations, plays, and material which you have. I think I'm almost as enthusiastic as you are yourself. I'm back on the line again. That means skiing and climbing as you put it. There's a lot more to this outfit than just that. I wish I could describe all the various methods of fighting which we will employ, but as usual, I'm rushed for time. Got to get up at 4:00 tomorrow as we are going through a course in village fighting which is about four miles from here. It is a very realistic course from what other fellows have said.

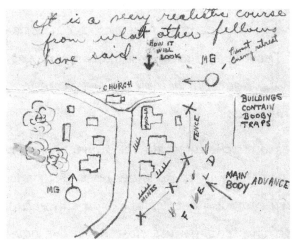

Ted's diagram of the attack course

How we attack it, I'll find out tomorrow. Several casualties have been reported during the simulated attack. You can see that we have, besides our regular mountain warfare training, training for all types of terrain.

I've been doing a lot of fishing in my spare moments. I never knew the Eastern Brook Trout would be found out here, but boy, I've caught some beauties.

I'm sure going to miss football this fall. I was planning on this year as being the year when I learned how to cut properly and use a change of pace. Lots of times I think over the chances I had had, but if I had only cut, I would have probably gone all the way.

I'm going to bring a ball back with me after the furlough. I go down to the gym when we're not on bivouac and play basketball and practice a little hand balancing. There are championships in every sport out here, so that I figure I'll be able to pick up a lot and keep in pretty fair shape.

Next week our schedule calls for more rock climbing, but we've already had some snow on the surrounding peaks. Every morning gets colder. You can actually pick the frost off the tent. I must close here. I've got about four hours to sleep.

As Always,
Ted

MY WRITING HAS BEEN DELAYED—THE SERGEANT KEEPS INCREASING MY RESPONSIBILITIES

Sept 25th

September 25, 1943

Dear Mom,

Furloughs were supposed to be opened today, but as usual they have been cancelled indefinitely. I'll get home someday, though.

I've been quite busy lately, spending most of the time participating in tactical courses which proved very worthwhile, I think. One course impressed me very much. We had to crawl at least 100 yards under machine gun fire and through barbed wire entanglements. The machine guns were adjusted for fire at approximately two feet. Also scattered about were fifty or so dynamite charges which were set off as we crawled along. The purpose of that was to accustom us to noises which artillery fire would make.

I've been pretty tired since we have been getting up from 1 to 2 hours earlier than the regular hour of 6

A.M. If you want to knit, I would appreciate anything, socks, sweater, wristlets, or gloves. Any one would be helpful. As for color, olive drab would be best.

Take care of Pop, and see that he puts out a good team.

Love,

Tink

September 28, 1943

Dear Gram,

What a wonderful package! Thank you! A little something like that is wonderful for the morale.

We're really headed into a long winter. It has already snowed several times. Our training is still summer tactics including rock climbing and mountain fighting.

This has to be brief. It has rained and snowed all day; therefore we must stand inspection at 8:30 P.M. And thanks to you for the rag. It does a wonderful job on my rifle and shoes.

I'm sorry I can't write more. I hope you understand. Thanks again, Gram. It was swell of you.

With Love,

Ted

P.S. No news about a furlough.

THE OLD MAN SAID AFTERWARD THAT IT WAS LUCKY I DIDN'T BUMP INTO SOME NEW SECOND LOOEY—

Oct. 4, 1943

October 4, 1943

Dear Mom,

I know that I have more than $28 at home. Remember I sent that in one lump. I also sent $10 and $15 other months. I need about 65 or 70 bucks. This is the first time I have asked for money. Maybe you don't think I've done very well, but there are lots of things you can leave out in your comments. I expect a furlough very soon so don't fail me. (Say maybe I should be writing to Pop... But I'm sure you are the financier.) Today we did some more rock climbing. It is one of the most interesting subjects we've taken up so far. I've been over some places that probably would have given you a fainting spell. We even practice how to fall. Of course, we do have ropes for support.

I went into Denver this weekend with Harry Wareham. He's a nice guy. We went to a dance and to the movies, "For Whom the Bells Toll". It cost me eight bucks round trip, 140 miles. I supposed I should have saved it but I've been sleeping in a tent too long so I took a pass. I left the air mail stamped letter back at camp. Good night.

Love,

Tink

UNITED STATES ARMY

October 16, 1943

Dear Gram,

I'm very sorry I've let my correspondence slip with you. We have been going at a terrific rate in our training and preparation for the inevitable.

I was very happy to hear that Nelda Louise is enjoying college life at Syracuse. We keep an infrequent correspondence but I do gather that she likes Syracuse just as much as I do. She has done nobly well in keeping me informed of the activities around the campus by sending me clippings from the Daily Orange. I think she is growing out of the adolescent stage into an intelligent young lady. Maybe I'm wrong, but that is the impression I receive from her letters.

I'm expecting another furlough in December but I'm afraid that it will come before Christmas. I am going to go with the next group, which would ordinarily be the 1st of November, but we are going on a month's maneuver next month and therefore all leaves will be cancelled. December 2nd is the date the next group will leave so you can expect me in Syracuse on the fourth or fifth. Remember that that date is not definite, but only probable.

This is just a short note to let you know I've been thinking of you a lot, and wish you keep you informed of my whereabouts.

Much Love,

Ted

Author's Note: *21-30 October - Ted's opportunity for a furlough must have come through unexpectedly.*

DATE November 3, 1943

HOUR 8:30 am

TEMP. 10°

Dear Mom,

When Phil and I got to Springfield, we did take the train number 57, but from Albany on, it was a Pullman train only. We changed at Buffalo and Detroit also. We came to a different station one hour earlier, in Chicago. We grabbed a cab and checked our bags in Union Station. Then we went over to LaSalle St. to meet the folks but we couldn't find them. I was more or less determined to see them, but how? I called all the Rautenbergs in the directory and decided to give up. I remembered, fortunately, that I had Aunt Mary's address with me. I hopped a cab and buzzed out 11 miles, almost to Evanston and finally got there after a half hour's ride. Aunt Mary, I found out, was down at the station waiting for me. I had the desk clerk call the station and have her paged. I was very lucky because that train (#57) was an hour late and they were still waiting for it to come in. I arranged to meet the three of them at the information booth in Union Station. They all looked just the same as the last time I saw them and Aunt Mary surprised me because she looked so well and moved around so spryly.

As soon as I reached the barracks I hopped right into my long johns as it was snowing heavily. Just to give you an idea of what we are wearing for every day work, here is a list: Long johns, knit sweater, O.D. shirt, heavy turtle neck sweater, ski pants, three pairs of socks (two heavy wool), shoe packs, parka, ski cap, and wool gloves with waterproof shell.

Last night our company was given a tactical problem of posting out guards to protect a bivouac area. Our position covered approximately 3/4 of a mile. We started posting our out guards at 7:30 P.M. I was out guard number one. My job was to challenge everyone by jumping out of a bush or from behind a tree and whisper "coffee" (sign) and If they did not answer "town" (counter-sign) I was supposed to bayonet or shoot him. Well along towards 11 P.M. two guys came strolling along the trail and out I popped. They jumped a mile. They gave the counter sign and they passed. Later I found out it was the Colonel and his right-hand man, the Major. They were the only challenges I really made but I did have a patrol which passed by every half hour. I was darn cold and tired by 2 o'clock as everyone else was. We got up at 7 this morning, five hours sleep. See what I mean? Lucky I have a few minutes to write.

Hope Mt. Herman won. How did Dolan make out? Oh yes, and Dixon?

Say hello to the Coach and Mrs., and Ryherts if you get a chance. Well I had a great time. Thanks for everything.

Love,

Tink

November 10, 1943

Dear Mom and Pop, (Killing a couple of birds with one stone).

I just received your letter, dated November 2. I think you left the A.P.O. number out. Don't forget to put it on the next letters.

It does seem like a dream being home. Boy, it sure was a short one, at least it seemed that way.

Well since I've been back, the company has been working on attack problems. It has snowed on and off all the time, so we use our camouflage uniforms. It is surprising the effect they have when you try to pick the men out while they lie in the snow. The company is split into two groups, one as the enemy and one as the attacking unit. We fire blank ammo in order to make it more realistic. My whole impression is that mountain attacking will have a much more difficult time than regular infantry units. First of all, we won't have the heavy artillery to back us up. Secondly, we have many more dangers than just our enemy. Thirdly, although we might find better cover and concealment in the mountains, contact will easily be lost. It's not that bad, remember the enemy is confronted with the same problems therefore only the best outfit will win, and you know who is the best.

Next Monday our ski training begins. That is really going to be some experience. Imagine living out in tents in sub-zero temperatures for a month! Just the same, I'm looking forward to it with unquestionable enthusiasm.

If there's anything more I dislike than doing laundry, I have yet to find out what it is. I have a lot of things piled up, too much, especially underwear. I'm on my last suit now. I guess this will be my weekend for washing my clothes.

I finally found someone who is going to take my picture for me. I'll send the film home and you can pick out the best ones. What I really want to do is have one picture taken in my ski outfit, have it enlarged and more prints made so that I can send them around for Christmas presents.

Ted in his 10th Mountain "whites"

Congratulations on a great season, Pop. You sure have an undisputed great team. Say hello to Bill for me and Sis also.

Well, good things must come to a close. Good night.

Love,

Tink

December 3, 1943

Dear Mom,

I was very sorry to hear of Uncle Ralph's (Rautenberg) passing away. Things sure happen quick. Are Chuck and Puss taking it OK?

There has been a great deal of sickness in camp, in fact there is no more room in the hospital so they are using up all the available empty barracks on the post. Every night we have to be in bed by 9:30 P.M. with shelter sides between each bunk. We still get up at 10 to 6 though, and we also have plenty of bivouacs. I'm in fine health, so don't worry.

How do you like Totsie's new car? A honey, isn't it? Have you heard from Betty lately? I haven't from her or anyone else, for that matter, for quite some time. I'm slipping on my correspondence but I'll keep 'em coming. Don't be impatient. I have received many packages from all the relatives including Aunt Dorothy and Hetty Hoyt. When I write to Hetty should I say Cousin Hetty, or what?

Every weekend I spend practicing skiing so that when we really get into training I'll be that far ahead. I've had several pictures taken, a couple in Kotocrom, which I hope will get back in time.

Today I was on a lumbering detail which was chopping and sawing a path from camp to Cooper Hill, 7 miles away. Most of the work has been completed so that it won't be long before we'll have electricity at Cooper Hill where we take our ski training. We are waiting for favorable conditions. Because the snow is not deep enough, we have been delayed almost a month.

The news looks very favorable, so it won't be long now — we hope!!!

Love,

Tink

Sat–December 11th, 1943

Dear Mom,

Sorry I haven't kept up on my writing but the days just slip by with my hardly noticing them.

Enclosed is a negative of me in the snow. You can have it printed if you want. I sent one of the prints to Betty and one to Gram Hoople. You've got the negative so you can do with it what you like.

I had those colored films taken almost a month ago but they haven't come back yet so I guess I'll have to abandon the idea for a while.

We've been out on bivouac for several days and it has been awfully cold. The average temperature was about 8 degrees during the three days. It hit 15 to 20 below during the nights. I'm still alive and kicking so everything is OK.

This is the seventh letter I've written today, so if you find it hard to read you can understand the reason.

How are you and Betty making out in your telephone conversations? Probably you've heard that she hasn't been getting any mail either. If you both can just be patient, I'll write but all the time I get letters asking please write or hurry up and write a letter.

Is Gram Rautenberg with you now? I received a check and a box of candy from Aunty Babe and Uncle Larry.

I received your packages too. Thanks a lot for the fruit cake. Boy it was a delicious one. I've got dozens of packages in my barracks back in footlocker. What shall I do with them? They're interfering with my daily routine because they're always in the way.

I think I shall treat myself to the movies tonight. If I can find time between lines and letters. Well, I'll close now.

With Love and Kisses,

Tink

P.S. Say hello to Harold and Alice for me. I just took the negative out and am having it printed here. Send it later.

Ted's Christmas card from Grand Junction, CO

Dear Folks,

I have been given a two day pass so finally I have gotten around to buying Christmas presents. First of all, I got both Grams a tablecloth which I thought would look nice on one of their living room tables. They are handwoven and about $5.00 apiece. Secondly, I have sent Betty a War Bond such as the one you have received. You should have another by this time. I thought that since you are about to receive another one, that it only seemed fitting that I buy one for Betty.

I'm sorry my Christmas shopping has been so limited this year. I only wish I could be home with you on Christmas day. Say hello at Uncle Ross's. Although I won't be there actually, I'll be there in spirit and thought. Pardon my mixed up sentences as I'm trying to write between conversations on the hotel bed. Oh yes, I forgot to tell you I'm in Grand Junction. The pictures ought to be back next week ($21.00). Happy New Year Too,

Ha Ha Ted

P.S. Up for a $4 raise.

December 25, 1943

Dear Mom,

I spent quite an eventful day today. First of all, I should like to tell you about the evening service at the chapel last night. Ten of us fellows went together and had a swell time singing and joining in good fellowship. We all talked of home and how each of us spent our Christmases in years gone by. After the service we came back to the barracks and talked over everything until 2:30 AM. We were very perturbed this morning when the C.Q. woke us up at 7 AM and told us we had to G.I. the barracks. After I cleaned up I opened up all the packages I had collected over a period of two months. The pants and wristlets will be put into use immediately. They were certainly a swell pair of gifts and most of all they are practical. Betty sent me a "ship the body" bracelet with my name and serial number on it. Gram R. sent me gloves as did Uncle Theo. Gram H. sent me a box of

Schrafft's for service men. A swell gift, everything from soup to nuts.

Dinner was ready at 1:15 and was it ever good. Turkey and all the fixings. I didn't mind the atmosphere too much because most of the boys were in good spirits. So everything went along fairly smooth. After dinner I laid down and mused for a while and then dropped off to sleep. This evening I went to the movies with the fellows and saw a wonderful picture that I want you to see. It's called "Lost Angel". You'll love it.

Aside from the above mentioned, today was just like another weekend day. Details were seen all around, especially the guard detail, KP, and C. Q's and firemen and so on, made the holiday miserable for some. I consider myself very lucky for not having caught any details.

It's all over now and it seems hardly true, but I feel very fortunate for myself because when I think of those fellows ahead of me, the next step ahead, I say to myself, you've got too much to be thankful for.

There has been tragedy up here in the last week. Two fellows have committed suicide by shooting themselves. It seems too bad that fellows lose their heads like that. I have no sympathy for people who haven't enough guts to take it.

That's enough of that. Well I presume that everyone had a swell time at Uncle Ross's. Boy, I sure hated to miss it, but I was thinking of you about the time you were sitting down to dinner. I wish my package had reached you but I just couldn't get over to mail it in time. Our three day bivouacs each week account for that and also my not writing so often.

Gosh, I sure missed you and Pop and Totsie, today. Happy New Year, Mom, and keep up the morale on the Homefront.

Much Love,

"Tink"

January 11, 1944
(after 3-day bivouac training)

Dear Mom,

I suppose Betty told you I called. I hope you're not jealous, are you? I realize too that I haven't written for a long time, but living in a tent, buried in snow at -30 degrees for a week and a half, just wouldn't permit me to write. I presume Betty hasn't heard from me either, has she, except that I called her up tonight and wished her a Happy Birthday. Do you think I'm wasting my time? You never say anything about her... or the farthest you go is "Oh she's a nice little girl".

Those pictures you have been so anxiously awaiting have not come back from the printing company. They were sent 4 ½ weeks ago. In that picture of me you'll notice that those wristlets have no finger holes or trigger hole. They are GI issue and not as good as the ones you knitted me.

I'm now back in camp attending snow jeep school. It's just the right time to be on skis now and I have to learn how to drive a snow tank. I'll be back up on the hill again in a week for three more weeks.

Did you hear Lowell Thomas? Well I was sitting in the audience. He sounds much better when sitting in the living room in the easy chair after a big meal. I'm in a moldy state with a long beard, but no hot water. So it goes.

Love,

Tink

Dear Gram, (Rautenberg)

All I need is just a little time to sit down and write. But at 30 below out on the ski slope, I haven't tried to write. You see, we've been living in tents continuously for nearly two weeks now. I just arrived back in camp in order to attend driver's school. I will soon be qualified with a snow jeep T-24. It does not have a steering wheel as the vehicle has tracks. It steers by levers not by a wheel, it is a four-seater with a heater.

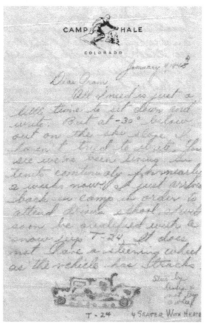

Ted's T-24 Weasel sketch on his letter to Gram

I am expecting some Kodachrome pictures to arrive any day now and when they do I shall see that you will have one.

Everyone is asking for a letter. At last I have a chance to answer a few anyway. I realize Uncle Ted and Auntie Babe haven't heard from me for a long time. It's a tough problem when you can't write and you should write. Even "the girl friend" (as you always say) hasn't heard from me, even on her birthday, but I plan to do something now that I'm back in camp.

Perhaps you heard Lowell Thomas, tonight. Well he was broadcasting 5 feet away from where I was standing. He sounds much more dramatic over the radio. He is a real skiing enthusiast accounting for one of the reasons for him being here. He said he was born and raised in this state so he must be some sort of sportsman. I use the gloves mostly for dress, as I think that is their purpose. At 30 below, we wear a mitten shell (waterproof) and two pairs of woolen mittens, and finally wristlets. The gloves are swell knocking around on the weekend, though. Boy, I sure like the way things are going right now concerning the War. Not too much longer. Gee, if you could only see the holes in my trousers and buttons. There are two things I miss very much. One is my laundry (on Sundays) and mending. Tonight is the first night in from the ski bivouacs for 1 ½ weeks so you can imagine how filthy I must be. Now, for a nice hot shower but there isn't any hot water since the whole regiment is out. How am I going to take a shower? Well, there are all sorts of little annoyances like that to make life interesting.

Thanks again, Gram, and keep a close watch on "the wolf" (reference to Ted's brother, Howard, Jr.).

Much Love,

Ted

Jan 15, 1944

Dear Mom,

Just a note to keep you going. Had a wonderful week with the snow buggies. Almost tipped one over while climbing a steep slope but tracks held us. One buggy did tip over though. The fellows didn't get hurt very badly.

The lights are just about to go out now. Hope you like the pictures, OK. The best I can do for now.

Howard wrote a nice letter. He sure sounds like he's enjoying the red heads now. Also heard from Aunt Babe. Sounds as though she's having trouble with the laundry. Haven't heard from Gram, lately. She and Gram Hoople will receive a large photo of me. I don't want to hear any complaints from anyone because they cost me $21 and $41 for the negatives. Sent lots. Uncle Bob etc., Uncle Ross etc., Aunt Babe, Uncle Ted, Aunt Mary, Jack and Bop each a small photo. Good night.

Much Love, Tinkle

23 February 1944 - The 90th Infantry Regiment leaves Camp Hale, but most of the men who trained there are transferred to the 85th, 86th and 87th regiments, eventually becoming the backbone of the 10th Mountain Division.

February 28, 1944

Dear Mom,

Well yes, I finally wrote the Johnsons—Betty of N.J. and Mrs. H.P. of Mass. Darn it, I realize that I am slipping but all this confusion up here baffles me and the irregularity of the situation doesn't help either.

Guess what I live right in back of Bill. Boy, has he got a nice girl. She goes to Bradford Junior College in Haverhill. I'll have to look her up if I get another furlough. I see him practically every day. It sure is good to have a relative around for once. I am now a steady weasel driver for the 87th instead of hiking on bivouacs. I drive, but sometimes I don't know if I like this softer life or not. When the 90th broke up, I lost my chance for a rating. I hope you're not too disappointed. I hated to leave that bunch because we had been together so long. Gee, we had the best platoon for cooperation and friendship I'll ever see. Well, I suppose I'll get in with another good bunch but I'll always miss that one.

If you like to knit, I do need a pair of mittens pretty bad, now. I also need some cotton undershorts (white!!)

oh yes, and some gray socks. Now, you asked me what I needed and that's it.

I'm having a little trouble with my teeth but they are getting fixed slowly but surely. Whenever I go to the service club, I always buy a quart of milk, which I miss very much at meals.

It won't be too long now before we'll be pulling out. I can sense that.

How are the applications coming in for camp? I'm anxious to hear about it.

The pictures have to be sent to the Rochester Kodak Co. N.Y. First of all you must get a price card from a drug store and then mail the negatives with number and the amount on them.

I'll write again soon. Until then take care of Harold and Alice.

Love,
Ted

March 4, 1944

Dear Mom,

There has been no definite settlement on furloughs. As soon as there is, I'll let you know just where I stand. It doesn't look too good now as we are ready for divisional maneuvers.

I see Bill quite often as he lives two barracks in front of me. If you look in the booklet, I can give you our general location. The service club is just one block north of us, a very nice location compared to most areas.

We've been driving, consistently, for other regiments on bivouacs. This driving is no snap. Two fellows fell off a cliff in their weasels.

Oh, ok, a new rumor hot from off the slopes. Furloughs might start in a week and everyone will go (drivers) at the same time. It's a pretty good one for once.

I'm glad you liked the pictures. I guess you thought I was bluffing all the time when I told you they were coming for about 2 months. Say, if you could find some Kodachrome film at a drug store I could find a camera and have a lot more taken.

It's still winter up here, not a sign of spring except around noontime when the sun climbs over the mountains. Then it is quite warm, but it doesn't last.

I went to a nice dance at the service club and met a nice girl (KKG Sorority) from Colorado College. It wasn't such a hot dance, though, too many in too little space and too few women. The band was GI and good, but much too fast for the Easterners.

I'm getting very anxious to get home again, especially so because spring is coming. Don't get me wrong, I like the snow and the mountains but it's been a long, long time since I've seen just a plain "ole" maple tree with leaves and took a whiff of Winthrop air.

What is Tots doing? I don't understand how they can grab him out of school. Did the Gillams get a chance to see him while they were there last month?

I received a letter from Aunt Ginny Rautenberg. Aunt Mary is staying with her in Evanston. I guess she's in pretty bad shape from what I gathered from her note.

The 87th has a swell regimental insignia; a picture of a mountain with a ski pole and an ice axe. Maybe I can draw it.

Hope you enjoy your stay in Oak Hills. Say hello to the folks. I'm kind of anxious to meet Mary my new step cousin. Hitting the hay, now.

Love,

Tink

Dear Gram, *(Rautenberg)*

Time goes by so fast I lose track of my correspondence. I didn't realize it had been so long since I had written. I doubt whether I ever thanked you for the candy, which I received some time ago. I've been switched around so much that it is hard for me to get settled enough to write everyone. I must say, Gram, you are my favorite oops, I've got to say both Grams because I've never had any complaints for not writing. I really appreciate your patience.

Bill Hoople lives several barracks from me and I visit him quite frequently. We have had some good times together, going to the movies and service club etc.

I am now a regular driver for the 87th. You remember I told you I was going to school? Well, now I am assigned to one myself. Don't worry about me. I'll be careful when driving. Besides they are not built for speed since they are cargo carriers. I enjoy that kind of work very much and I'm with a swell bunch of fellows.

I mailed a letter to Totsie. As I don't have his new address, I sent it to your house. Would you please forward it to him? I suppose he is getting good marks in his subjects, living by himself where he can do his work.

It looks like spring is on the way up here. The snow is melting fast and the days are getting much longer.

I haven't been able to hear Uncle Ted on the radio (station for the Sunday night Cleveland Symphony Orchestra concert broadcasts). Would you send me the information as to how I could hear him?

Mother wrote me a nice letter from N.Y.C. where she was enjoying herself with the Gillams and Johnsons. I wonder how the camping business is going to be this year.

It's time for chow so I must close.

Love,

Ted

March 15, 1944

Dear Mom,

I have received your latest package of underwear of which I was very surprised to see so soon. I thought I mentioned it before, about the two previous parcels. That stocking cap is a corker, especially when we are sleeping out in the field. I wish you would pick up more of those socks. They are exactly what I wanted and the size is perfect.

Betty sent me a huge box of brownies. She claims she's a lousy cook but I can't convince her that they were great.

I've been having dental work done since the middle of February. Oh man, those docs don't have any sympathy for teeth like mine. They always complain when they catch me as a patient because they have to work so hard. I've got a little book with all their names in it, so I can campaign against them after the War. "Brutal that's what I calls It!"

Driving takes up all of my time. It seems like every officer and his brother wants a weasel. When they get me for a driver, I'll give them a ride rough enough so that they will hesitate before they decide to ride instead of walk. Today I went over to the gas station and loaded her up for tomorrow's bivouacs. It only took 22 gallons, bet you could use some of that. Ha, ha, ha.

I'll let you know, but quick!! when I get a furlough. There's no use in making any statements because there are none, except that it will be in the near future as long as they are still open.

I never saw two women fight for a letter from me any harder than you and Betty. What is it that attracts your attention?

I suppose George is still making rooms cloudy with his nickel smoke generators (cigars). Gram R. sent a dollar enclosed in her last letter. Pretty nice!
Well another rough day tomorrow so---oo!!
Love, "Tinkle"   P.S. Is Totsie really in the Army?

March 19, 1944

Dear Mom,

I can't remember how long it's been since I last wrote so I guess I'd better get on the ball.

It's my ninth day of my second year of going into the Army. Incredible!! How have I lasted so long?

We leave next Saturday on the forever talked about maneuvers. That will mean plenty of work for the drivers as far as the 8-hour day is concerned. We have been lugging cargo for the past two weeks. Of course I think it's easier than packing a rucksack, but I would still like to be with the old gang again.

I haven't heard much news from Betty. Seems as though she must be studying pretty hard. Hey, what's the dope on Totsie? Is he just going down to Upton to get his uniform? If he does get back to school, he's going to have a pretty rough time from what other fellows say about their friends who are in A.S.T.P. They say you must really have a liking for medicine to go through with it.

This is rather a skimpy note but I just thought you would like to know I'm in good health and think of you a lot.

Much Love,
Tink

26 March - 6 May D-Series Maneuvers, designed to test the division's ability to operate in the mountains in subzero weather, push men, mules and machines to the limit of their endurance.

Sat. April 1, 1944

Dear Mom,

I received your airmail letter in the middle of last week while I was on the first series of maneuvers. The 86th is still here and as far as I know we will move out all together and I think it will be quite a while before we do.

This past week has been the coldest week of any so far this winter. Tuesday, 25 below was about the day's average. Hundreds of fellows were sent back to camp with frostbite and frozen hands and feet. A whole division camped out on a snowbound mountain with nothing but the Weasels for communication. That is the set up, so you can see the importance of drivers. I had some exciting experiences myself as I was broken in as a blackout driver. Some of the embankments we nearly went over would make your hair stand on end. Several of the Weasels did dump over but luckily no one was injured. Boy, I got really tired around 3 AM, but after that I seemed to be OK and pretty fair the next day after no sleep. During the whole week I slept only once and the only way I could do it was to hide. I slept for 15 hours straight. I guess it was about 3 or 3:30 in the afternoon when I woke up.

We have just today to get cleaned and washed up before we start out again tomorrow at 5 AM.

I will need some cash for furlough, which you can send any way you think best. I don't think wiring it would be the best way because there would be no way I could get it while I'm on maneuvers. I expect to get it the later part of this month.

I just received the gloves and socks. They are absolutely swell. Just the equipment I am short of at the present. Thanks!!

Give my regards to the Dunhams and tell Alice she should see the West—wild and woolie!

I'm losing plenty of weight on these maneuvers as is everyone else, so don't be alarmed if I seem kind of slim below the solar plexus.

Much Love and a happy Easter,
Ted

April 3, 1944

Dear Mom,

I'm afraid you wouldn't recognize me with a beard! Boy, it's a honey. Today has been nice for a change except that it was mighty cold during last night. I haven't had a good night's sleep since that 15 hour snooze last week. I feel pretty well and eat as regularly as possible. Night driving is tough but I can manage OK.

Say, did you hear that my friend, Chuck, is going to be home around the 20th. Oh, if I can only make it. I'll have to see the CO and explain the situation to him.

I received a card from Warren Bazergan, who is now in a "zoot suit" also. He's taking his Basic and from there goes to cadet training school for fliers.

Not much news today—haven't had any mail other than the socks and gloves.

I just hope I do pull a furlough soon.... *(Last page of letter missing, written on April 4, 1944.)*

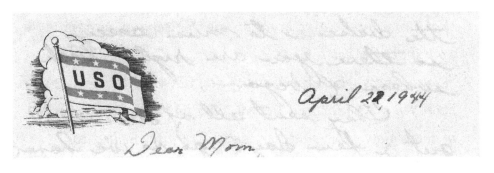

April 22, 1944

Dear Mom,

Well I just can't understand what's so confusing about getting furloughs in the army. I'm not even sure of getting one in May, so please don't make any plans that would interfere with business. I am undecided as to what to do when I reach Syracuse. Should I stay over a day like I did on my last furlough, or should I come straight through? I am very anxious to get home for once but if you think I should stay at Syracuse I will. Write me what you think. Relatives are sometimes a hindrance, when you want to get home in a hurry, but I hate like the dickens to miss seeing them. So, there you are, right back where I began.

They sent all of our Weasels out a few days ago, so we haven't much to do. The Maneuvers are still going on, only on a much smaller scale. The boys can come back to camp each night until 11 PM and then they must report to the bivouac area.

I am trying to get a ride to Denver this weekend so that I may make a reservation on the Zephyr, in case I do happen to get a leave.

Say—Guess who I meet every day down at the service club? Niome Minot and Penny, who has quite a number of teeth now. She said her folks were just thrilled to have you and Dad at Mt. Hermon, and that they miss you very much now that you have left. Niome is a swell girl and her husband is a pretty nice fellow also.

The boys from the motor pool had a swell time at a dance last night. We stick together like glue as we are the only newcomers in the Regiment, and feel a little out of place with the rest of the outfit. We had a perfect system. First we would spot the belle of the ball and tag her. With 8 or 10 fellows, we danced with her all the time and occasionally we brought her into the lounge and talked a while. You can imagine how embarrassed she must have been when we started to kid and joke with her. A good time was had by all.

When I get home, the first thing is to get me a dental appointment as I need one quite badly. I've tried to make one here but they take patients by regiments and our regiment is all through, so it would be about June before I could get one. There is just a little more work to be done as I have been going since the last of Feb.

Haven't heard any news from Totsie, so I guess he must be very busy studying. I hope he likes it. You asked me about his being a PFC. Well they are automatically made a PFC when they enter and besides that they are paid about $75 /month, I believe.

It never stops snowing. In fact we have had more snow since March than we have had all winter long. I imagine by the middle of May we might see some fair weather— but you never can tell. I sure hope the camping business picks up or has by now. I've been quite concerned about it or interested you might say.

Say did you know Vince Gauss was in Company I 87th? He was a frat brother at Syracuse and was just recently transferred up here from an infantry training center right near Jack Braunig. A small world, no doubt!

I expected to hear from someone on Easter but not a soul did I hear from. I was with Bill most of the day as we were resting a day from maneuvers. I taught Bill a little something about driving a Weasel behind the army's back. A lot of fun. I'm running rather short of news so I say good-bye and here's hoping. Love, Tink

April 24, 1944

Dear Mom,

I sent a couple of letters home before I received your letter saying that you were leaving for Syracuse. There's no use in planning because I don't know whether it will be a week or a month before I get home (most likely a month).

Please don't try to arrange or postpone any business on account of me. I'll follow you as long as you let me know just when and where you'll be. Ole Betty has been asking for a letter—well I guess I do owe her one after two weeks but the maneuvers and all make letter writing a real problem. We are still out in the field, but we are able to get passes and come into camp from 5 to 10 PM. If I only had a washing machine, my troubles would be over. I have more dirty clothes than I could ever hope to bring home. Oh gosh, and holes the size of silver dollars in my socks.

What's the latest dope on Syracuse and I hope the applications have picked up since I have last heard from you.

I met a Marine from the Naval Convalescent Hospital in Glenwood Springs, who was from Syracuse. His Uncle or cousin runs McCarthy's Seafood Joint near Sears and Roebuck Co. He's been through the ropes, I guess. Still snowy.

Much Love,

Ted

Received your check—Thanks!!!

Card to Nelda from Mrs. McManus, Glenwood Springs USO:

April 22, 1944

Dear Mrs. Hoople:

I am very happy to report that your son, PFC Ted Hoople was a guest at our USO center, last Saturday evening. He was very tanned and seemed quite well and happy. We were glad to have had him with us.

Mrs. McManus, Hostess

Written on the back of the card from Mrs. McManus from Glenwood Springs USO:

April 24, 1944

Dear Mom,

On pass at Glenwood Springs. Looks very doubtful whether I will get a furlough. Boy, I'm becoming more anxious every day.

Love, Ted

April 26, 1944

Dear Mom,

Today is the first day that has the "makings". The sun has been out all day and it has been almost hot outside. In fact it was so warm I had to change into my summer underwear.

I went out on the range this morning and fired the transition course over again. I just qualified as it was pretty cold early this morning and my hands nearly froze trying to load a clip of bullets. I believe we will move back into camp by the middle of next week which will be a relief to all of us. My clothes are filthy and in terrible condition—I'm lost!!!

I see Bill once in a while but he doesn't have much to say. He looks well and seems to have weathered the Maneuvers quite well. As for myself, I weighed in at 183 with my clothes on yesterday, so you can see I didn't do too much strenuous work as far as physical activity was concerned.

Well, just a note, but something to keep you going.

My Love,

Ted

Dear Mom,

Here's a clipping I found in our newspaper and I thought you might be amused by it.

Just received a letter from Totsie and he didn't say anything about you or Dad being in Syracuse. He must be overloaded with work but he claims he's going to take a weekend off and come over to Boston on my furlough. He was trying to tell me about the dissection of the body, which nearly turned my stomach.

Yesterday, the motor pool went through the close combat course. The buddy system is used on that course, so Doc Greene, a Cal. boy, and I went together. Instructions were to pass up a small draw until you reached a clearing just beyond the aspens and there take up a firing position on enemy positions you might see. Our first obstacle was concertina barbed wire. Doc crawled through while I covered him and then I crawled through and he covered me. We crawled into a small ditch from there and tossed a hand grenade out in front of us to clear the assumed enemy in foxholes. After the explosion we charged out and bayonetted two surprise targets on our flanks. We advanced a few more yards before we made a mistake. Instead of going around a log bridge four feet from the ground, we went across it. Boom!! A stick of dynamite went off below us. My head was surging the rest of the day. There were several more barbed wire entanglements, surprise targets, and booby traps before we arrived at our firing position. We had 16 rounds or two clips of 30 caliber ammo to fire on various silhouette targets. That was the final phase of the course. One thing that really bothers me is that it is very easy to shoot your own buddy if you don't take precautionary measures.

I would like very much to have a furlough. Be careful of Howard now and don't tantalize him because he has plenty of work to do.
Beautiful blizzard today. I hopped right back into my long johns so don't worry.

Much Love and a kiss,
'Tinkle
P.S. Haven't heard from Betty lately. Kind of peeved at me for not writing I guess.

April 29, 1944

Dear Mom,

Well here I go again. I've just been transferred to I Co. 87th for no reason I can visualize. I'm of course upset and disgusted, but I'm getting used to that by now as you can easily see. The first thing I did today was to see about a furlough and the result was not too favorable. I'm going to work on it until they tell me to go away. I think I explained the situation of furloughs in the 87th. Most of the boys have not had a regular furlough in 1 or 2 years, but remember they did have 20 days when they got back from Kiska, so you can judge for yourself how things stand with me.

I sent a large bundle of dirty clothes to Denver to be cleaned. I hope I get them back soon because I am in urgent need of clothes.

Well, I hope my next letter will bring you more pleasant news than this one. Sorry to hear about Howard and his women, but he's just fooling around. He never goes with one long enough to get serious.

Good luck with camp. Until you hear from me again, much love from your son,

Tink

May 10, 1944

Dear Mom,

Very sorry to hear of Gram's illness but I'm happy to hear she recovered quickly.

I was coming home the 16th to surprise you but somehow they said that the other fellows should go before I do. At the rate (7%) of this outfit it seems as though I'll be here a very long time indeed.

I'll never be sure until I reach the front door so have a ready to eat lunch in the ice box between now and December.

With all the moving around I've done up here how the heck can a guy get a break? I'm looking for just one break now, and that's the war.

The company's having a big beer party in the mess hall tonight. Steaks and fried chicken included, so maybe I'll be able to forget my worries for a while. The company is spending about $700 on the party, so I should imagine there will be plenty for all.

That's wonderful news about the camp. I just hope it keeps progressing in the same manner. Say, thanks for sending those Daily Oranges (Syracuse University daily newspaper). I've enjoyed reading them in my spare moments. I sure want to go back after the war, if it is at all possible.

I haven't heard any news from Howard at all, but he better come to Belmont when I do get a furlough.

Bill and I are going over to Aspen this weekend to visit some nice girls he met last year. Don't worry about my spending that money. I haven't even cashed the check yet. All the money I spend comes from my monthly pay. Say hello to Gram for me, and Pop.

Much Love,

Tink

15 May 1944 - Ted gets a two-week furlough and goes home, stopping in Syracuse and Cleveland to see relatives on the way back.

May 27,1944
(Cleveland Heights, OH)

Dear Mom,

I am wondering how you and Betty made out after I left?

I really can't begin to tell you what a wonderful time I had, in what seemed like the briefest two weeks I've ever experienced. But I do know that I did everything I had planned including seeing friends and having my teeth fixed.

Ted at home on leave with his brother, Howard, and his parents

Boy, I sure felt miserable the first few minutes after we said goodbye. And that wasn't all. I said goodbye to Gram Hoople, Pop, Auntie Babe, and Uncle Theo in the short space of 15 minutes.

I am now at 2222 Belfield Ave where everything seems to be going smoothly. Gram looks fine but still works too much and Aunt Crucita, like you said, is practically helpless with her swollen arm, but she does manage things quite well in spite of all the troubles. The Simmons dropped in tonight and I spent a dull evening listening to a black market oration by the Mrs.

I leave tomorrow morning for Chicago and from the looks of things, I will not have time to see the Chicago Rautenbergs.

Well my line is slowing down. Thanks for a wonderful time. It couldn't have been better unless I was home for good.

Much Love and Kisses,
"'Tinkle"

May 29, 1944

Dear Pop,

How's the boy today? I sure had a tough time leaving Friday. They (the 2 girls) practically had to shove me on the train. I realize my coming home cost you a small fortune and I want you to know that I really appreciated it and that someday I shall be able to repay you in some form or another.

I had one wonderful time, every minute of it. I can't believe it's over yet, but I might as well get used to facing realities, now.

I arrived in Cleveland around five thirty and had a grand time with the Rautenbergs even though it was very brief. They all decided that I should take the 11:20 instead of the 8:00 to Chicago. Well, it didn't take much persuasion as I was pretty tired and I needed a good rest. I arrived in Chicago just in time to catch a cab and make the Streamliner at 5:45.

I see the Braves won a twin bill from Chicago. Keep me posted, will you?

Good luck this summer. It looks like a great year. Thanks again.

Your Son,

Ted

P.S. I wrote this letter on the 29th but since we were out on a two week trip, I did not get a chance to mail it.

4 June 1944 - In Italy the Fifth Army breaks the Gustav Line and enters Rome. North of them, the Germans regroup and establish a new line of defenses across the mountains named the Gothic Line.

6 June 1944 - D-Day. With the Allies' assault on the beaches of Normandy, Italy becomes, "The Forgotten Front". North of Rome, the Germans fight rear guard actions to allow time for the fortification of the Gothic Line, which stretches coast to coast, north of Florence, across the crest of the Apennines. Breaking through these mountain fortifications and exposing the soft under belly of the German occupied territories in southern Europe is a daunting task that calls for the specialized troops of the 10th Mountain Division. The next five months will be spent finalizing training, equipping and mobilizing the 10th to spearhead the final assault.

Dear Mom,

How are you? I've lost all track of your age. If you don't get some gray hairs pretty soon I'll have to call you my sister.

Did Pop take you to the ballgame today? (Ha, ha). Anyway, I hope you had a Happy Birthday. Maybe next year I'll be there to make it a very happy one.

It's pretty definite that we are moving to Texas sometime this month. That's about all I can say about the whole thing because I don't know any more about it than that. Strange, don't you think? I'm sure I wrote you a letter from the Rautenbergs' establishment. You never said anything about it.

Say, I think that your graduation gift to Betty was super. How did you happen to think of it? I laughed for 10 minutes. That was a perfect inscription, don't you think? Very tactful, indeed.

I wonder if you have heard of a Diplomatic family from Corning, N.Y. by the name of Heath. Their son is in I Company and from what I gather he is a well-known society person. I happened to mention him because he, George Geiss, and I went on a pass together to Colorado Springs last weekend. It seems that "Heater" has a future wife in one of the coeds at Colorado College. Boy, what a swell campus and women at every corner but George and I only went out to visit the college life and compare it to Syracuse. We both approved but we still have a prejudiced opinion and I feel that Syracuse is tops. The chimes at Colorado U. were the first thing that we ran into, but the sound wasn't nearly as voluminous and clear as the Crouse Chimes. I can't think of anything more pleasing to a weary guy, than to throw himself on a green lawn with a maple tree shading him (and listen to those chimes). That's just what we did as soon as we hit the campus. "Heater" took his girl out that night so George and I went to see "Snow White" once again. We also went on a sight-seeing tour of the Broadmoor Hotel for a little recreation. While we were there we went swimming and horseback riding. It took me off my feet, financially but I figure it was worth it. Maybe I'll get serious minded someday and start sending money home. Happy Birthday, again. With Much Love, 'Tinkle

P.S. I forgot to mention a girl we met out at Colorado College. Her name was Roberta Scholsser from Evanston, Illinois. And she knows of Bill Rautenberg. Quite a coincidence, I think.

When are you leaving for camp? Let me know so I can write to you promptly.

Say hello to the Dunhams for me. I think Alice is sore at me for some reason. Do you suppose she disapproves of my courtship of Betty or is she jealous? (Make sure she reads this) (ha ha ha)

TRAINING, CAMP SWIFT, TX

Ted in his "khakis" with 10th Mountain patch

June 29, 1944

Dear Mom,

Heat, heat, and more heat!!! Arrived at 10 AM this morning soaking wet. Took about 3 showers so far and I still smell like a dead fish.

For reasons that I don't know, the address Mtn. Inf. must be changed to Inf. We are still specialized troops in a class by ourselves. I guess it is for military reasons that the Mtn. is to be dropped off.

I have an idea that we won't be here too long. Either that or we won't last long in the heat. This is a pretty location with numerous swimming pools and service clubs. Its capacity is about three or four divisions. It reminds me of Fort Devens.

The various units I have seen training here are carrying little infantry sacks while we lug around our new jungle packs (smaller than the rucksacks but on that same design.)

I received your package of food and opened it on the spot. Everyone in the barracks came over to help me eat. We were all famished as we had not eaten since this morning at 6:00 and it is now 2:30 PM.

We spent about two days traveling from Camp Hale. We rode east as far as Newton, Kansas and then headed directly south for Texas, passing through Oklahoma City and Fort Worth, which I did not see as it was my turn for the upper berth that night. I cannot figure out how I can have the address changed other than having my dog tags changed to Medomak, Maine instead of Belmont. If I do tell the C.O. he'll forget, anyways. A lot of fellows are confronted with similar problems which are insignificant to any of us, but I guess it seems quite important to you, though. All I've heard is what I don't do and the mistakes I've been making. Boy, I got awful mad when I was expecting a nice letter from home and then find one full of criticism. Enough said about that.

Boy oh boy was it ever hot!! The last night I spent at Camp Hale I nearly froze with my overcoat, gloves, and ski cap on. I was driving all night. From one extreme to another. They will either make or break us.

I'm going for a long swim tonight, believe me.

Thanks for the package, food, and stationery, and pictures. It was swell.

Say, I think I can pick you up one of our sterling silver regimental insignias which are better than the ski pin, I think.

From your well broiled son, much love,

Tink

Dear Folks,

Fourth of July is here again but no sign of celebration is evident. I received a card from Gram Hoople with some money in it. She never seems to miss anyone when it comes to Birthdays or Christmas. Betty sent me a silver dog tag chain because she didn't approve of the string I was using. A swell gift, I think. Uncle Ted wrote me a nice letter, sending his best wishes to me and giving me the low down on the Cleveland clan.

Man!! Is it ever hot. I'm shaking the sweat off my arms right now. In order to cool off every night, we (Brad, Pete, Ernie, etc.) go swimming over to the pool. I've been practicing a little diving lately, which I find has been sort of a relaxation mentally. I've been working on a Gaynor and the 1½ forward dive. This camp seems to have twice as many recreational activities as Hale did. It is almost like coming back to civilization again.

I was particularly impressed by the green vegetation when we arrived here. Pictures of the desert and sage brush kept flashing in my mind before we got here. It certainly was a surprise to see trees and grass around. I had also counted on a terrifically high temperature, which would have been almost unbearable. It certainly hasn't felt as hot as I had imagined, although it was 120 degrees Sunday noon. All in all, I am in favor of this move. The change has been good for all of us.

Haven't heard from Totsie in a long time, not even a Birthday card. Is he disowning me?

(I just had to remove my shirt because it was beginning to stick from sweat.)

War news looks very good so I'll say goodnight. Thanks again for the snacks.

Much Love,

Tink

July 5, 1944

Dear Uncle Theo,

This outfit sure takes the cake for seeking the most difficult climates to adapt oneself to. Last Sunday, two days after we arrived, the temperature reached about 112. The night we left Hale I was driving a jeep, checking the barracks, and before I was through I was wearing a field jacket under an overcoat plus a pair of gloves. None of us can quite fathom just what the reason was, but we have some pretty fair guesses which seem to hold weight.

Are any of the Rautenbergs in Cleveland going to be able to make Cranberry Lake this summer? I would certainly hate to see those fishing holes down in the bay go to waste. Maybe by next summer I'll be able to make it. War news looks more favorable every day.

Although I spent only one day at 2222 Belfield Ave. I certainly had a wonderful time seeing all the folks again. I was extremely fortunate in seeing all the relatives I did, but I did "flub the dub" in Chicago and I really got the "dickens" from Nelda.

It was great to hear from you again. Thanks for the nice letter. Gosh, I haven't written to Gram in a long time. I had better write her a few lines tonight. I think she has arrived at Cranberry by now, so I'll write to her there.

For recreation on my free time, which is quite limited, I go over to the swimming pool and practice diving. It is a swell sport and it also helps to relieve the mental tension which is created after too much concentrated training. I've heard the Pops Concert a few times but it is rather difficult to get near a radio to make it a regular practice.

I'm hitting it up pretty strong with my woman but I'm sure nothing will develop until after the war. Mother sometimes gets a little worried about it as it was quite evident while I was home.

Johnnie (Rautenberg) sure impressed me as a live wire. We had a great time that Sunday morning I left. Went racing out to the park and all the time he pumped me full of questions. Glad to hear Teddy is doing a good job helping out at home. How did the elections come out? As I remember he was "sweating out" the returns. I was very sorry to hear that Aunt Crucita is not coming along too well. That's a tough break. Hope she pulls out of it soon.

Don't over-do on the sports. As Mother puts it "You're burning the candle at both ends." I knew you were a tennis player but matching a champ never entered my mind. (ha ha)

Give my best to all the clan including the dog, a much better improvement over Rondo. He (Rondo) used to give me a very hard time at Cranberry, remember?

I'll close by thanking you again and I think of you all very often.

Much Love,

"Hoople"

July 7, 1944

Dear Mom,

Enclosed is a picture of the Weasel which we used this winter and on maneuvers. Just recently it was made known to the public. How do you like the looks of it?

I haven't been able to purchase one of our regimental insignias yet, but I can promise you one soon. I suppose if

Betty sees you with one, she'll want one too, so I guess I'd better figure on two but yours will come first.

You mentioned something about Chuck Herald being in Texas, but you didn't mention what camp he is in. If by chance he is in Camp Hood, which I think is about 100 miles, I might be able to see him on a prearranged engagement.

I am planning on going to Smithville on a pass tomorrow. These small towns around here are full of cheap women and girls that are just looking for a chance to rook some soldier. Don't think I'm not well informed on that subject and furthermore don't worry about me. I think I have had one of the finest bringing up of any guy in the Army (don't get conceited now). But anyway, I thought I would just like to straighten out a subject which I've hardly ever discussed before because I know you've probably wondered just what my viewpoint has been on that subject, since I have been in the Army. Besides that, I think I have a pretty darn nice girl at home and my conscience would bother if I had ventured into the lower type of pleasure (so they call it) and I know how she would feel about me. I don't know if I'll ever get a chance to marry her, but at least I would pick a girl as high in character as she is, in my estimation.

Well Mom, I'm sure I set you straight on a few things which we have hardly ever discussed and I hope you approve of my very stolid resolutions.

I'm very sorry to hear about Aunt Mary and I feel worse about not seeing her this last time. When I last saw her she was apparently in excellent health and that is the way I would like to remember her. As soon as I get a chance I shall write her a letter. Darn it all, I've got so many letters to catch up on, I feel lost.

Glad to hear camp is really lively. "The more the merrier," I always say. The war news continues favorably, doesn't it?

Time for me to get some sleep for ½ hr., we are going to run a ½ hour cross country course tomorrow so Goodnight.
Much Love,
"Tink"

July 14, 1944

Dear Gram,

I can just picture you and the whole family seated at the table eating fresh trout and drinking that cold spring water, which I would give $5 for a drink of right now. I presume you are still seated at the head of the table with commanding view of all the goings on at either side. I'll never forget how angry you used to get when I tipped my chair back. Has anyone carried on the habit where I left off? Hey Gram, how 'bout a letter from some of your granddaughters, especially Mary, whom I have not heard from at all. I shall imagine that the male situation over at the village is almost extinct by now. Certainly that would give the girls more chance to write even if they do spend most of their time trying to tan themselves or comb their hair. It certainly is a good thing that there are a few men there to take over and control confronting problems which continually arise. Does the hammock still hang from its prominent corner on the porch? I hope that no one has misused it for a swing, like Totsie and I used to.

Yes, my longing for Cranberry has certainly grown stronger, especially down here where we are under a continual heat wave from sunrise to sunset. Now to get back to reality. We have been put to the test in this heat. Yesterday we journeyed for 12 miles before lunch. It wasn't too hot but there were quite a number of fellows who suffered from heat exhaustion due mostly to their own fault. They did not take the necessary precautions which were continually suggested before we started. This is certainly a most peculiar spot for ski troops to be. Maybe they are figuring on training for sand skiing. At least there is plenty of that around here. I definitely think we have our mission assigned to us, but don't let any of that stuff fool you, I can be just as wrong as the other fellow. At least it looks like we will be here for quite some time to come. The only bad news from the war comes from China but still considering our small forces and insufficient supplies we are doing very well over there. I use "we" because we are all part of one, when you really think about it.

My time is running short, now. Above me hangs a sign which reads "Deep in the Heart of Texas". I only wish it read "Deep in the Heart of the Adirondacks".

Much Love from your Grandson,

Teddy
P.S. give my love to the mice on the mantle.
P.P.S. I forgot to mention the main purpose for writing I'm sorry!! I was so deeply concerned about what I was writing that thanking you for remembering my Birthday utterly slipped my mind. You have never missed me yet. How do you do it? Thank you. Hoping to hear from you soon and the sun-bathers also.

Give my love to all,
Theo

July 25, 1944

Dear Mom,

Maybe I can explain why I haven't written. Yes, its heat all right combined with a tough schedule this month. Last night we left our bivouac area at 11 PM and by 4 minutes to 1 AM, we had covered nine miles. Figure out the energy spent and maybe you can see how we have been going. 4.5 miles per hour is a fast walking pace but remember we have about 40 pounds of equipment on our backs plus rifle, helmet, etc. This morning we took it easy for once. Tomorrow we are supposed to do 25 miles in 8 hours or less. Say, if you come across any light weight hammocks I would appreciate your sending it as we are going to be on this bivouac two weeks more. After a few days in camp we'll probably start out again. I've made myself a makeshift hammock out of my shelter half. It hasn't rained since I've been down here, so I think I'm fairly safe tonight.

Yesterday afternoon, Eddie Meyers and I walked across the road, over a grassy hill to a watermelon patch. I filled my pack and fatigue jacket full of watermelons and cantaloupes. It sure was a big pack but I didn't realize it until I tried to lift it. I had to drop a few out as much as I hated to. Tonight I still have 3 watermelons left. I'm afraid the whole patch has been cleaned out by now.

Last night after we finished the hike and checked out, there were 5 of us left out of the original 40 in our platoon. Strange as it is, every one of us came from New England.

It's going to be more and more difficult to write so forgive me if I slip up now and then.

Haven't heard from Betty in quite a while. Wonder how she's doing with her job?

Must get on with my sleep now.

Much Love,
Tink

August 8, 1944

Dear Mom,

Thanks for writing so often—Sorry I can't say the same for myself though. Glad to hear Dad's weekend went off so well. You certainly must be having quite a time with so many people around. Pop ought to be an expert at juggling ration points by now.

We came in Saturday after two sweaty weeks in the field. Can you imagine how smelly I was having not had a bath in 13 days?

George Geiss, Brad Rousseau and I went on a pass over the weekend to Austin. We were extremely fortunate in purchasing a room for three, near the Texas U. campus.

It was like coming out of a hole into the sunlight. My, but the co-eds are pretty down here. We spent most of our time at Barton Springs just outside of town where most everyone spends their weekends. The water is very cold. Something we have been looking for since we arrived.

I saw Bill out there and we had a little chat. He receives quite a bit of my mail now and then. This time he told me he had a box which was mailed as a Birthday gift. Tonight I finally got my hands on it. It was—you guessed it—a box of chocolates, fairly mutilated but nevertheless edible. It was from Aunt Dorothy. I'll bet she's angry with me for not writing.

I wrote a nice long thank you note to Gram R. but I omitted thanking her until after I had written the closing line. I turned the paper over and explained that I was deeply interested in what I was writing so that I would have to thank her with a P.S.. Evidently she missed it when she received the letter. Night Problem (training exercises) tomorrow.

Much love from,
Tink

August 13th, 1944

Dear Mom,

Just came back from a long day out on the (no not the field) the golf course. I've played about 4 times since I've been down here and have improved very gradually. I think the first two times I shot around 135 or 140 but now I've cut that down to the low twenties (123 to be exact). I've got the well-known golfer's bug. My trouble is that I can't get it straight about the fairway and the ruff. The fairway looks pretty easy but I always play it in the ruff. Bob Dudley (36-year-old), I think I mentioned him several times before, is a very good player at his age. He shoots very consistently in the low 80s.

I wound up my week-end with a lovely reddish-brown tan since I was only wearing a pair of shorts while playing.

About the regimental insignia, I have had them ordered since March. I was in H & S Company the other day. I went over to see about them but it seems that the fellow who handles that work is sick. In the meantime, please don't get discouraged.

Next month the division is going on maneuvers in Louisiana for two months. As far as details on the whole thing, I am in the dark but will keep you posted. That hammock you spoke of would really come in handy.

Out for the whole night again—Am getting ready now.

Much Love,

Tink

August 22, '44

Dear Mom,

It seems as though you just got to Medomak when I received a letter stating that camp closes today. Gee, another summer has passed already, or it has nearly passed.

Thanks ever so much for the Maple Sugar. I never did care much for it until I opened the package. On the cover it read 100% Pure Maple Sugar, Newport, Vermont. Just the sound of Vermont tasted good. Quite a number of the boys are New Yorkers and New Englanders so you can imagine just how long it lasted. I read in the paper today where Syracuse will play Boston College on Oct. 24th at Fenway Park. I wish you would try and take Betty to the game because I know how much she enjoyed seeing Dolan play at Herman.

Maneuvers have been temporarily cancelled so by October I presume we will be singing the Louisiana lullaby. How is the hammock coming along? I certainly would be grateful to you if I could have it, because you know how much I enjoy snakes and insects crawling over me at night. Last night I shared my foxhole with several small spiders and numerous ants.

Glad to hear Gram is going to be with you for a while. I owe her a letter, which reminds me I also owe Nelda and Mary (Ted's cousins) one. I received Howard's insurance papers by mistake. They are the forms dealing with the auto accident and they must be signed before the money is turned over to him. I believe the balance is about $10 and some cents. I'm sending them back, right away. Well, here's to the end of the War. Bottoms up!

Love,
Tinkle

September 10th, 1944

Dear Mom and Dad,

Please excuse me for not writing in the past few days. I received your package with the hammock, which arrived just at an opportune moment. After supper Tuesday night the mail was distributed and I was ever happy to see it. We were out all last week.

About those insignias, I have been over to H & S Company several times without any results. Last March I paid $3.40 and have heard nothing more than come back later when they have more time so that the records can be checked. As soon as I have a few spare moments during this week, I will make the attempt once again. Be a little more patient because I have not forgotten. I can hardly believe Nelda Louise is going to Syracuse this fall. If you really would like to see her in Alpha Phi, I don't see any better move than writing Gloria H. and G. Howe. She does not have any friends, probably, and the first ones she will be acquainted with, if they are any good and they are, seem to have more influence than other ones. I wrote her a week ago and told her in a joking way, as I always do, that the Alpha Phi's and the Sig Ep's were not on good terms. Maybe I did the wrong thing, you might say, but I think the psychology is perfect. As time goes by, I am beginning to wonder just what kind of adjustment will be made for fellows like me, who were dragged out before they ever had a fair chance. The point system of demobilization for most servicemen is a fair and reasonable scheme, but they forget the younger guys who have not had a chance really. Dependents and overseas service, according to the point system, ranks first. I say overseas duty absolutely comes first and I doubt whether anyone else would disagree with it. But the mustering out of men with dependents doesn't seem quite fair because most of them are older men who have had a fling at life and education. They are mostly married and have children etc. In general, we who want to go back to school, feel there is some neglect on the point supervisor's part because they don't seem to realize that we are the builders of tomorrow and maintainers of peace. If we don't get our chance soon, after the war, I'll venture to say that during a period of 5 years, if these fellows are left out in some army camp, 90% of them will say "I'm too old to start school" or "I'm too far behind the times to spend four years at schooling". Please don't misunderstand me; I do realize how difficult it is for a woman to manage on a small allotment from the government. The percentage of fellows is probably too high for anything to be done about it. Let's get the war over with first!!!

Perhaps if I tell you about last week you might be able to see why my letters are so well spaced. 5:30 AM Monday morning, we packed up, had breakfast, and crossed the IP at 7:30 AM. We marched 4 miles to our bivouac area, in silence mostly, as the fellows were wearing off a rough weekend the hard way. Immediately we set up a tactical bivouac area and "dug in" (foxholes).

At noon we pulled out two dried up sandwiches, which we carried with us, and drank as much water as we had left in our canteens. The afternoon was spent on lecture classes; 1 ½ hours each on the 60-millimeter mortar and the .30 caliber light machine gun. At 5:15 I went on guard duty. I was through at 9:15—a long day but longer ones came later on during the week. Tuesday morning, we left the guard post at 6:30 AM and were driven out to the company area. At 7:30 we were oriented on a "problem" and issued 8 rounds of ammunition. It was 800 yards long but mostly in the open field and that meant that we had to run and drop every 3-5 seconds. Targets would appear every so often and that would give us a breather. The sun gave us no mercy while we pumped lead as we lay on our stomachs. We completed our problem at about 1 in the afternoon. At 3PM, after dinner, we went to a demonstration which showed the tremendous firepower in an organized defensive position. Machine gun, rifles, mortars 60's 80's 75's and 105's proved their value in covering every advancement. Near the end it rained very hard. After supper I went back to my area to sleep but the rain had made a roaring torrent of water out of it. Dudley and I spent a lot of time digging drainage ditches and building a large campfire after the rain let up. Wednesday morning at 6 AM I rolled out of my hammock feeling like a worn-out dish rag. At 7:30 we fell in and started on a 20 minute cross country run. At 9 we surveyed our bivouac area and mapped it out using a compass and covering every inch of the area. By that time, we were ready for dinner and a rest in the afternoon before a "night problem". We checked over our equipment, cleaned our rifles, washed and shaved. It was a GI rest alright. It clouded up around 4:30 and began to rain with full fury. I was due for K.P. Thursday so that meant that I would not have to go out on the night problem. I had to get up at 1:00 AM and help the cooks with the sandwiches and coffee for the boys. At 2:30 I dropped off to sleep again only to be awoken at 6 AM just as the boys were coming back. Although I was going through hell, I didn't envy them in the least. A sorry, sloppy, soaked company straggled by the kitchen in twos and threes. After lunch the order came through to pack up and be ready to leave at 2:30 PM. Most of the fellows did not have any sleep since the night before as their equipment needed immediate attention to prevent rust and rot—another so called GI rest period. The kitchen was loaded on trucks but we marched along with the rest. It lasted for 5 or 6 miles and then we were informed of an imminent attack from the "enemy" (85th or 86th). We set up the kitchen and fed the boys in the dark. The meal was already prepared by the cooks before we left. By the time we finished dishing out the grub there were a few pickles and a slice or two of bread left. We completed our K.P. duty around 11 PM. practically 20 hours steady but I still did not envy the rest, as they were out all night on patrols. At 5 AM we began an attack (this was Friday morning). We continue until twenty- five minutes of six in the afternoon. We carried all of our equipment with us so that when the problem was over, we could march back to our original bivouac without going back after our equipment. 8:00 PM, we pulled in, hungry and thirsty (two sandwiches and a very light breakfast). When we arrived, there was no kitchen in sight and then griping began (only the best soldiers gripe anyway). In a half hour the kitchen arrived with a hot meal in kettles and pans. Food doesn't seem to make much difference when a guy gets thirsty. I mean we were really dry because our canteens weren't filled that morning, due to an oversight, purposely or not by the higher ups. After bloating ourselves we settled down beside a small campfire and sang a few songs. Most of them were the swell harmonies, like "Swing Low" and "Old Mill Stream". Then there were one or two modern ballads such as "I'll Be Seeing You" (that is really one of the best today, try it out—that's a must). Of course, a few fellows made out with a so called "smutty" song and there were some hearty laughs. I made an acquaintance with one of our Lt.'s. His name is Earl from Syracuse '37. Said he had Uncle Ross for Philosophy and that he should have gotten an "A" instead of a "B". I think he said he was a PHI SI or something. George Geiss, Earl, Burns, and I sang the "ole Alma Mater. "Where the Vale of Onondaga etc." Burns recently joined this company a few weeks ago. He left Syracuse last December with Harry Wareham, Jack McClusky, Perry Smith and quite a few more. We could certainly have quite a reunion, don't you think? I'm getting a little off from the story. After practically falling asleep, we finally broke up the party to get some shut eye. Saturday morning, we got up before the roosters, 4:30 AM, in order to break camp and be in the barracks for chow at 7AM. The rest of the morning we spent in cleaning and arranging our equipment and taking a written test on trench foot. Passes were issued at 12 noon for 50% of the company. Those who did not go out on pass fell out at 1 PM for organized athletics (this is the last sheet of paper. I hope you haven't tired of this detailed description). Dudley and I took the football, which had softened up during the week and hiked down to the field to get it pumped up as the company was lacking in those particular facilities. We still had enough pep in us to get at it "hammer and tong". We won something like 6 touchdowns to 1. It was a fairly cool day, as the sky was overcast and for once in our favor.

Perhaps you wonder why I haven't been to chapel very much. Well I slept right through until noon today. Do you find fault with that? They should hold service Sunday afternoon instead, I think. I went to the movies for a little entertainment this PM. I was very delighted with "Arsenic and Old Lace". An old play that was in Boston for quite a while, remember? We had a swell dinner of creamed chicken, string beans, mashed potatoes, lettuce salad, lemonade, and ice cream. A whole day of relaxation apparently was too much for us so we prepared for a little game of football an hour or so before dusk. I'm tired now and feel like kicking myself, as does everyone else that played. But it was fun and took our minds away from that incessant GI atmosphere. I have now scribbled up to the present moment where I am seated at a writing desk in the day room, which is about to close (11PM). Next week sounds much more inviting with 3 night problems instead of one. "Woe is me!!!" Here's to victory darn soon!!!

Much love and a kiss or 2 for you Mom,
Tink
P.S. The candies were enjoyed by all. I started to re-read this for mistakes but I quit at the fourth page. Read with an open mind, please.

September 18, 1944

Dear Mom and Pop!!

Did you have a wedding anniversary sometime this month or is it next month? I received a "Messenger" and noticed Jean Kelly is already married. My goodness, how awful!!! She used to be such a swell date and a lot of fun.

Received one letter from Totsie over the weekend. The two "Nans" it seems are running a hot race, neck and neck. Of course, Howard told me to keep it "under my hat" but you can see how small my overseas cap is. Really though, he's just letting them fight it out between themselves. He's a card if I ever saw one.

Your eyes will pop when I finish describing the recent three day pass I was on. I left camp Friday morning around 8AM. The company was lined up out in the field, opposite the barracks doing calisthenics and close order drill. With a wave and a smile, I was off to the capital of Texas (pop. 87,000). The first thing I did was get a room at a private home for $1.50 for two nights and all the fixings except meals. After that I stuffed myself with a good dinner at a Spanish cafeteria. Later I met a couple of boys who were also on a 3 day pass. We spent quite a long time, in fact the best part of the afternoon chumming with the waitresses at the USO Club. We found out that Austin High School was playing New

Bramfels High in football on Friday night. Of course, we sat on the Austin side but we cheered for New Bramfels thus making ourselves quite unpopular. Someone hollered out "Them damn Yankees!" I turned around and a sweet old lady with her grandson sitting beside her asked what part of New England I was from and I told her. Well, she had lived in Lowell during her childhood and finally ended our brief conversation with "I guess we're both damn Yankees" and told Bobby, her grandson, to shove over so that I might sit down. The stadium was way overcrowded. They really go in for the sport down here. Austin won 27-0.

While we were walking home after the game a car drove alongside of us just as we were about to cross the street. A girl poked her head out the window and asked us where we were going. We were nearly overcome by surprise but quickly ended further discussion by saying "home to bed". That was actually the first time a woman has scared me since I was 11 years old. That was M.B. Morrison when she washed my face with snow and chased me home. I don't think you knew about that because I wouldn't have told you then for anything. Well anyway, getting back to the subject. It must be the war, funny world.

Saturday, we slept until noon and showed up at the same cafeteria again. All the time my finances were moderately dwindling. I went over to the lobby in the Alamo Hotel and waited for Dudley, who was supposed to meet me there. While I was waiting, I listened to the Michigan vs. Iowa football game. I was also supposed to meet George Geiss at the Servicemen's Center at 7PM. I finally met Dudley and told him about George so he said he had something lined up and we'd play golf the next day. I waited for George, but he didn't show up. Several of the other boys did and we decided that Texas U. needed a few boasters at the Saturday night dance. We danced a few but it was the regular GI routine of step, tag, step, tag, etc. I bought a milkshake and went back to the house and to bed. The next morning, I was after Dudley so the first place was the USO. We met him as he was just coming out the door. I told him to wait a couple minutes while I checked my bag inside. While I was inside, a fellow tapped me on the shoulder and said "Hello, Hoop". For a few minutes I was racking my brain for this fellow's name. His face was very familiar, even his voice. Finally, with embarrassment I had to have a little help. It was Stillman Copp (class of '46) and played guard on the freshman team. We had to delay the golf game for a few minutes so Dudley went out with the intentions of meeting me out at the clubhouse. All during that time I couldn't figure out where George was. Finally, I said so long to Stillman and headed out for the golf course. It wound up like this. I couldn't find Dudley or the other guy so I started back to town. I dropped into the USO again and there, glory be, was George! It was around 12:30 PM Sunday. George had met a very nice family who had invited him to spend the weekend with them at their home, which I gather was something. The two of us put or heads together and said I, "Let's try a Sorority". OK says George, you call them. After quite a bit of persuasion, I gave in. 2244 was an easy number, Alpha Phi by the way. Somebody answered and I told her who I was. Then the hot air flew thick and fast as I explained about Syracuse and how congenial they were up there, etc. etc. etc. One thing led to another and before we knew, we were ringing the doorbell. The first girl we met had a pleasing personality and rather eased the entrance of the rest of the girls as they came casually tripping down the stairs. At one time we had as many as ten of them in there listening to the experiences of two great mountaineers, ahem!! They finally let up on the questions and ushered us out onto the patio. It was a lovely sight but a pair of panties, hanging from the porch rail, added a slightly sour note. When it was finally discovered by the girls, we were quickly ushered back inside again. We had so many to choose from that it was rather difficult to ask any particular one for a date so we waited around a little longer. During that time 3 or 4 would leave and 2 or 3 would enter. Finally, we did end up with two dates made to order. Then I began to realize how embarrassed I would be if I didn't make the financial ends meet. We journeyed out to Lake Austin for a boat ride and a few dances at the Austin Inn across the lake. The girls had to be back at an early hour for studies. We moaned and groaned to ourselves but that was that. I ran into a strange coincidence with Margie. Her mother was Alpha Phi and her father was a Sig Ep. Well, "You all think that's pretty good"?

Said goodbye to the girls and of course politely asked for a return engagement in the near future. Of course, the reply was just as favorable, "You all come back soon?!!" Mmmm. We were back in camp around 9:30 PM and so we took in a show to make things complete. "Since you went away" was the title. It's a woman's picture. Don't miss it.

I have written these lines from the bottom of _____ my _____ foxhole. Give my regards to Uncle Frank (Poland). Hoping you all are well.

Lovingly, Tinkle

P.S. The next you receive, just fill in the missing words & you'll understand what I have written. Besides reading the letter you can play a game of "Fill in the Word" or "Can you Connect This?"

25 September 1944- Headlines in the New York Times highlight the breakthrough of the Gothic Line, achieved at great cost by the Fifth Army fighting along Highway 65 and Futa Pass. The article hints that a breakthrough to the Po Valley is near. In the central sector, the penetration is in fact carried to within 8 miles of Bologna, But the weather is horrible, troops are exhausted, and low on supplies. American commanders are fearful of the artillery defenses that General von Senger has massed around Bologna behind the high peaks of the Apennines.

October 3, 1944

Dear Mom,

I am expecting a furlough in 4 or 5 weeks at the most. You can never count on a thing like that. We might start maneuvers in November and that might stop furloughs, but the set up now is in my favor by a long way.

Last week I went to the University of Texas and Southwestern football game, which in my estimation was a very poor demonstration for what this Southwestern Conference football is cracked up to be. Of course, there's the old argument, "the war". Still, it was very lousy.

This week I have a very good deal. I have working hours from 8PM to 12PM. The rest of my time is my own with which I can catch up on my letters and sleep. Nelda Louise wrote me and sent me this clipping of Eddie Dolan. I told her before she went there that he was going to be a good player. She has certainly been around though. Chi Omega, Tri Deltas etc. etc. She did not seem to play any favorites. I wonder what sorority she will pick.

I haven't heard from Howard since the last time I mentioned him. Where did he spend his leave?

I wish you would send me my basketball shoes as quickly as possible as we are having a company team. Please do that before anything else.

Oh yes, I forgot to thank you for the peanut butter fudge. It was delicious, and I would like about 2 lbs. of it. How about it?

Much Love,

Tink

October 30th, 1944

Dear Folks,

I had decided to wait for you to settle down in one place before I would write again. We've been hitting a terrific pace down here due to so many inspecting officers from the corps area. We are, as you know, going on maneuvers the 5th or so of this next month. Unconfirmed reports say they will end the 2nd of Dec. at which time I will start on furlough as I am the first or near the top of the furlough list.

I presume Betty enjoyed the game Saturday. Too bad about the score. The Team is having some tough luck this year. I know Betty would have cheered for Syracuse if I had been there but Joe Elliot and a few other Bostonians caught her fancy. How is Joe coming along?

Last Thursday night company I's basketball team journeyed to Austin High School where they played a practice game with the "Maroons". Frankly we were badly beaten. During the first half due mostly to lack of practice and little or no coaching, team play was very poor. Too much bunching in the bucket, sloppy passes, and slow cutting were main faults. The kids were very fast and I think, judging from their play they could take any Middlesex conference, hands down. Our team consisted of Joe Colone, center 6'4". He played in the Penn State High School Championship. (I think he is capable of playing better than average college ball.)

Tom Burns was playing at right forward. I believe I have mentioned him before. He's from Binghamton and went to Syracuse in '43. He stands at 6'2", is good under the basket and also a good shot. Lee Allen, another Syracuse kid (6'1") played guard smoothly. He played at Peekskill with Pellegrini, Shifter, and Simmons. He was headed for Syracuse but the war interfered. Lind played the other guard at 5'10". I could see that he had played basketball before and I found out later that he was from the University of Washington. I played left forward but I'm sure I saw better days in high school. I can still move as fast as I ever was but I couldn't shoot "for Beans". Next Wednesday we are going in for another practice game. Since last Thursday we haven't seen a basketball. I think that our lack of practice is our main weakness. The Captain has given us every break possible but that amounts to about 2-3 times a week. Today and tomorrow we will be constantly on the alert for the inspecting officers, so you can see how much practice we're going to get. Nevertheless, I think we'll take them. During the coming winter we have games scheduled with all the neighboring high schools. The boys get a big kick out of playing and beating a service team so consequently everyone wants a game.

I received a letter from Bill Burke. He figures he'll be at least 2 more years in the Pacific. I'm inclined to agree with him.   Much Love, Tink

6 November 1944 - The 10th Light Division is renamed the 10th Mountain Division and reorganized as a "Modified Triangular Division". Each of the three regiments (85th, 86th, and 87th) has 12-line companies, including one heavy weapons company in each battalion. The men have been intensely trained and robustly conditioned over the past 18 months. They are prepared and now the Division is streamlined to mobilize and enter the fighting with their special skills.

November 7, 1944

Dear Mom and Dad,

I think they're using stage coach for mail carrying lately, don't you? Really, I'm sorry. What can I say?

This is election eve. First of all, I might say that if I were voting I would stick with the Elephant's party. I suppose because of your influence, but I think that Dewey is a very capable man. One thought that I don't quite agree with though is his foreign policy in regards to Russia and the Lend Lease Bill.

I can just see how the Bridge Game is coming along-ha, ha. I have forgotten almost everything I had learned about Bridge.

Sunday, we left camp at 2PM with packs that went well over 50 lbs. When we arrived at our bivouac area and finished setting up defensive positions, we were ordered to stand by, to repack, and on maneuvers instead of 30 days! Whew!

Saturdays we have compulsory athletics which includes tackle football in fatigues. During the game last Saturday, I skinned my arm on a cement sidewalk, ran my tooth through my lip, and received a solid charley horse. We had a swell time, really (won 6-0).

Our address has been changed again. We are once more "Mountain Infantry". Probably tomorrow it will be changed again. Until then, Mountain Infantry will be the correct address. Going back to athletics again, last Wednesday we played Austin High again and this time we won, 36-32, without a single practice during the time between our previous engagement...

Thanks for the fudge. It has made a big hit with the fellows. They all say that you, Mom, are a good cook. Who am I to argue against that? Today we are leaving on a three day battalion firing test which should prove very helpful to us because it gives us an all-around picture of what combat will be like—at least it will be the best picture possible.

I've met a very nice girl, June Mower, who goes to the University of Texas. She has attended Pilgrim Fellowship Conferences in New Hampshire, Michigan, and Ohio. She hails from a small town near Amarillo. Since I was expecting a long maneuver, I took her out to the best places, bought the highest priced steaks, and attended many dances. I was out for a big time and boy was it! I'll tell you more about it when I come home on furlough again. I have no idea when it will start. One moment it is December, the next it is November. Keep your fingers crossed and knock on wood if you are superstitious.

Just heard that Dewey has been defeated. I guess your Bridge party did not pan out so well. Better luck next time. It's only 4 years from now. Roosevelt is practically the only president I can remember through my life. I do remember the first time he ran against Hoover in '32, I think. Totsie and I had a Hoover pin on the observation car of our electric train. It doesn't seem so long ago, does it?

Well here's to a quick victory!

Love,
Ted

A letter home from brother, Howard:

15 November 1944

Dear Mom,

Thanks for the letter. He sure sounds a little bit homesick, so I wrote him—it's about time I did. I wish you'd send me more of his letters so that I would feel like writing to him. I don't expect that he should answer mine, but the ones you get should serve me too. About those pictures. I just haven't had time to go and get them done but I'll see when I can do it.

Love,

Totsie

P.S. Election night made me think of the same Hoover button he speaks of. In fact I felt psychic at the time. How funny!

17 November 1944 - The division's assistant commander, Col. Robinson Duff, arrives in Naples to make plans to Move the 10th Mountain Division to Italy.

24 November 1944 - In Italy three battalions of the Fifth Army, supported by tanks and artillery, make an unsuccessful attack on Mount Belvedere. After briefly gaining the summit, they are forced off by accurate artillery fire directed by German observation posts on 4,600-foot-high Riva Ridge. The ridge is 12,000 yards long, west and south of Mount Belvedere, overlooking the village of Querciola in the valley. After the repulse of these Fifth Army attacks, General Von Vietinghoff directs that the German defensive position on Mount Belvedere be redesigned and improved. Mines, trip wires, and concertina wire were laid across every attack approach; farmhouses and small towns are fortified; artillery and mortar fire are set up; and aiming coordinates registered. Nothing has been left to chance as the weather hints of the coming season. This final line of German resistance defending the wide-open Po River Valley is ominously named the "Gothic Line". The future of the 10th Mountain waits as the winter of 1945 settles in.

Elite German mountain troops display their confidence and Edelweiss insignia

29 November - The 86th Regiment leaves Camp Swift by train, arriving at the Port of Embarkation (POE), Camp Patrick Henry, VA on December 2.

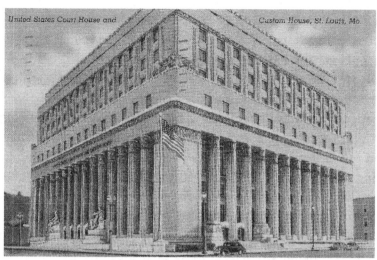

Postcard from Ted's 3-hour layover in St. Louis

November 30

Dear Folks,

Have a 3 hr. layover here in St. Louis. Saw "Howie" and "Nan" at the station. Thanks for a wonderful time while I was home. Even though I did run into a number of difficulties, being home was the thing that counted most to me.

It is very cold here—around 25° I believe. Met a few of the fellows and am walking around town taking in the sites.

Love,
Ted

THE ALAMO

December 4, 1944

December 4, 1944

Dear Mom,

Your Thanksgiving package was waiting for my empty stomach when I arrived. The box was in poor shape so some of the boys fixed it by eating the cookies, which they said were delicious. Your Toll House cookies lasted a little more than ten minutes, they went over really big. Most of the fellows have received similar packages all along so you can see we have a continual supply coming in to aid the morale.

The train stopped for 20 minutes in Syracuse and Howard and Nan were there to greet me. I guess Gram Hoople was too tired to come down. Howie says he'll be home for Christmas. At least he convinced me because I made quite an issue of it. Nan kissed me goodbye. I think she's trying to plug the deal through me. Really though, I think she's OK for my money. But from now on women, to me, all of them, are creatures to be handled delicately and never to be considered seriously, (ha, ha)! The rest of the trip was uneventful. If it was, I was too tired to notice it and further more I had too much to think about.

Today we are playing Bergstrom in Austin. Most of us just returned from furloughs and are in poor condition without any practice. I still think we can beat them if we click like we did against Austin.

I believe we'll be in Texas a while longer than I thought. One of the first things I noticed when I arrived back here was the 86th had left. Too bad McPherson didn't get home. If I had been in that regiment I wouldn't have either. There is a certain amount of luck in the army, I think. Bye for now.

Love,

Tink

11 December 1944 - The 86th embarks for Naples, Italy on the USS Argentina. They arrive 11 days later on Dec. 22. The 87th would soon follow. As soon as the troops are aboard ship, their pay is increased 20%. For example, P.F.C. Hoople's pay would be increased from $54.00 to $64.80.

December 15, '44

Dear Mom and Dad,

We've been pushed pretty hard this past week, completing our final training in the States and drawing new equipment. Yesterday we "GI'd" the barracks and laid out our entire equipment for a showdown inspection. It's interesting to note the fellow's reactions within my acquaintances. Some of them are excited and anxious to move on. A few, very few I've noticed, develop sudden ailments which when examined would wash them out for overseas duty. I am proud to say that none of my more intimate friends have turned color. Others are concentrating on training which they feel they are behind in. The majority appear nonchalant or show a "take things as they come" attitude combined with an uncertain feeling.

No, I did not see the almonds but I heard they really hit the spot after the turkey dinner. I received your Christmas package yesterday and had to open it immediately. Everything in the box arrived in excellent condition and I did not have to discard any of it. I passed out the lolly pops and the boys thought it was a big joke but the fact is they disappeared quickly. Thanks for so many useful, well sorted gifts.

We've played three basketball games since I've been back. We lost all three but we were never outclassed. Our first game was with Bergstom Monday night after I returned from furlough. Seven of the other players were in the same boat I was. We played well until the last quarter where our conditioning was lacking. We faded out and threw the ball away most of the time. At the end of the third quarter we were leading by 5 points and then we went all to pieces. The final score was 46-37. The second game was almost identically the same, Austin 45, we were 40. Our final game was played here in camp, against the Camp Hale Post Champs. They 46, we 39. Aside from our poor showing on paper, I think with proper training and good coaching, we could compare to any Jr. College or small University.

I don't think I'll be able to write again until I arrive at P.O.E. Here's hoping to see you again before I leave. I'll try to call anyway.

Sure am going to miss Christmas again but I will be thinking of you constantly. It has been quite a number of seasons since we—all of us—have been together on Christmas. Let us all hope the next one will find us together again.

Until later, love from your GI Joe, Tink
P.S. Merry Christmas

21-24 December 1944 - The 85th and 87th Regiments are moved by train from Camp Swift, Texas, to Camp Patrick Henry, VA.

ITALY, 1945

4 January 1945 - The 85th and 87th embark from Hampton Roads on the USS West Point bound for Naples, Italy. The ship was formerly the USS America, largest and fastest of the U.S. commercial fleet. Too fast for any convoy, it sails alone, unprotected from German U-boats, until it reaches the Straits of Gibraltar.

8 January 1945 - the 86th enters the front lines north of Bagni Lucca, relieving battle-worn troops in the Mount Belvedere area. The Brazilian 1st Infantry protects the right flank. The left flank is essentially open, with 25 miles of mountains between the 86th and the nearest Allied unit.

8-11 January 1945 - General Hays flies to Naples and immediately travels to Traversa where he meets with General Truscott, commander of the stalled Fifth Army. Truscott says, "My plan is for your division to first capture Mt. Belvedere and then proceed to capture all the high ground to a position east of Tole." Hays replies, "Who is going to share the bullets with us when we attack?" Truscott answers, "No one." The capture of Mt. Belvedere is key because it provides the Germans with unrestricted artillery observation positions over Route 64, one of two main approaches to the prized Po Valley. General Hays soon decides that an attack on Mt. Belvedere would be successful only if the German positions on Riva Ridge were neutralized. Riva Ridge overlooks Mt. Belvedere and gives German artillery spotters a clear view of the whole area of Mt. Belvedere. He assigns the endeavor to take Riva Ridge to the 86th.

Dear Mom,

Through the courtesy of Bill Essilinger, I am able to write you just what has happened since I left Swift. Bill comes from Belmont. He graduated a year later than I did but I do know him pretty well. I was walking through the companionway the first day out. I saw a tall sailor in front of me who looked very familiar, but I was unable to recognize him. At once, I saw his name stenciled on his shirt and I knew who it was. We talked over Belmont for quite some time. Finally, he told me that if I wanted to write a letter, he would mail it for me once he reaches Boston after the return voyage. This explains what I am going to say and why I am able to write it.

(**Author's note:** apparently this letter, by design, would not be subject to censorship if carried to Boston by Essilinger and then mailed.)

When I returned from furlough, we were still training in field work and very little time was taken for movement preparation. Gradually the situation reversed and I could see that it was about time for me to give you a ring. The same afternoon after the call we had a retreat formation at which time it was announced that we were restricted to our company areas for 36 hours. Then we would move out. We spent three full days on the train passing through Louisiana, Mississippi, Alabama, Tennessee, and finally Virginia our P.O.E. state. None of the southern states impressed me in the least. One of the places I was a little "stare crazy". It was the crossing of the Huey Long Bridge near New Orleans. Once a day we stopped and took time out for calisthenics. I remember our exercise in Chattanooga, Tenn. particularly. We stopped in the freight yard and ran around boxcars for a half an hour. Tiny Phillips and I were partners in Bridge against our two sergeants. We trounced them completely. We had won two rubbers and were well on our way to a third before they even made a game. That was our first try and we continued to do it the rest of the trip. We arrived at Camp Patrick Henry on the 22nd of December. The camp is located some 25 or 30 miles southeast of Richmond, near Newport News. We were actually told that after a week there we would all receive passes for 72 hours. Christmas Day I was up at 4:30 AM, only that certain day I was put on the army's most delightful detail... K.P.!! Days dragged by and New Year's was gone before I realized it. Our physicals and other last minute details having been cleared up, I was all set for a pass. Then came our 72 hour notice which meant just 72 hours left in the States. A day later, at 1800 hrs. a lot of soldiers stuck their heads out of barracks windows and doors. The guy in front of me wisecracked a little but I know most were enjoying their last few steps in the States. It was 9:15 when we reached the pier. There wasn't a blackout but the dock and warehouse were dimly lit. I was having quite a struggle with my pack, B.A.R., and duffle bag which totaled about 160 lbs.

Consequently, I did not notice the Red Cross girls who were passing out hot cups of coffee. As I passed the examiner's box I was under a bright light. We were instructed to sing out our first name and middle initial after they called our last name. The

(Timeout!!! 8 days out and land is sighted.

The Rock of Gibraltar is on our port side)

light confused me and I was slow in replying. I was then walking up the gangplank and that is where I took my first look at the SS America, now the USS West Point. It was formerly the largest luxury liner of the United States. We poured into our compartments in a steady flow. Our hold was just aft of the starboard bow. We bunked three high. On other places on the ship I have seen them crammed 5 and 6 high. We did not sail, however, until the next morning. I took a good look and went below for breakfast. We passed several fishing boats and one or two warships. Once a school of porpoises jumped water, one after the other. The seagulls or whatever they were did not stay with us long. I was constantly on the lookout for our escort but evidently a ship of this size and speed does not need an escort except in extreme cases. There are approximately 10,000 men on board so you can imagine the responsibility the Navy has. During our second, third and fourth days out, the water became quite rough and the number of seasick cases was unbelievable. Tiny, Brad, and Ted Reinero* never left their bunks for at least four days. On the fifth and sixth days the weather calmed down somewhat and the decks became crowded once again. I like the sea and only wished I could have experienced a real storm. Today we sighted land and from our starboard port we judged that it must be Africa. It was several hours before we reached "The Rock". I was playing Bridge at the time and therefore took only one quick glance from the porthole on the other side of the ship. We are now moving into the so called "Blue Mediterranean" bound for Naples, Italy. The weather is rainy and visibility is very poor. We have just picked up a corvette and destroyer escort of six or eight ships. Several Navy patrol bombers have been cruising around us. It gives one a sense of superiority to see such protection. Tomorrow night we should be in port and from there to a training camp of some form or another for intensive mountain training, best as I am to judge.

Well Mom, just a word more about this. Please dispose of it as soon as you are through with it. This is my last attempt to send any information like this. I thought it over and decided that it was a good opportunity to let you know a few facts.

Time for me to chow up at 3 PM. We eat only two meals a day.

Much love always from a jolly would be sailor,

Tink

13 January 1945 - The USS West Point arrives in Naples, Italy with the 85th and 87th at 4:30 PM. The next day, they head north to Livorno by rail, freighter and landing craft.

15 January 1945 - The newly arrived troops bivouac 3 km outside of Pisa.

20 January 1945 - By this time all three regiments are on or near the front lines Between the Serchio Valley and Mt. Belvedere. General Truscott's desire for the 10th to spearhead the advance into the Gothic Line is taking shape. For the next three weeks, the line companies conduct reconnaissance and combat patrols, some of them on skis, while the commanding officers plan the assault on Riva Ridge and Mt. Belvedere.

January 22, 1945
(Front lines, Serchio Valley)

Dear Mom and Dad,

This is my first real opportunity to write to you since the boat trip. I am in Italy and I would like to state with great emphasis that this country is in ruins, especially the towns I have seen. The Germans are so systematic and thorough in their destruction that I for one cannot fathom how the populace was able to survive through it or continue to survive without our assistance. During a train ride, in a box car no less, I was able to observe the people and their way of life as compared to ours. It is quite obvious that they have gone through Hell from the grim appearances on their faces and how grateful they seem when we pass them pieces of candy and biscuits from our rations. Most surprising of all is the pricelessness of cigarettes. They are a more common medium of exchange than money. Even young boys of nine and ten years smoke, so you can imagine the value. As far as the physical appearance of the Italians, actual starvation is not commonplace; I have seen several cases of homeless children begging for their existence. Their swollen feet attracted my attention. Apparently, they haven't had any shoes for quite some time. This is more common in the cities. Somehow the rural folk are better clothed and look healthier than the city people. As we travel through one section of the country, I failed to see one house or building that was not destroyed beyond repair. All along the wayside the Germans left a great deal of equipment. Tanks were left just where they had been knocked out. It was a very desolate countryside and I was more than happy to be going through.

Yesterday we (the platoon) took a hike up a winding road, two miles to a monastery which was established about four or five hundred years ago. The architecture was of the old Gothic style. It was a massive piece of work which probably took many years to build.

The only thing I can mention and feel safe in doing so is that we are eating exceptionally well, far better than I expected.

I would like just two things to be sent. First, a pocket knife, a very handy instrument. Secondly, a football, which I would like most of all. Every time I try to get the company's ball, they haven't got it with them or somebody's using it. Probably I won't be able to use it as much as I would like, but when I do have a few spare moments, I enjoy tossing it around.

Tell Howard to write, as well as Jack. I am desperate for some news about you and your activities at home. How's the bridge coming along? Tiny and I haven't made out so well. We've been overbidding too much.
Until I am able to write again I remain your loving son,
Tink

28-29 January 1945 - The 85th and 87th Regiments relieve the 86th on the front. The 86th is given the task to assault Riva Ridge in the coming weeks. This requires extra training in mountaineering and reconnaissance patrols in search of possible routes up the 2,000-foot mountain wall. The 87th holds in support mode, securing as much local territory as possible.

Dear Folks,

Just a short note to inform you of my well-being.

The weather has been so constantly miserable that we have been allowed to board in the natives' houses. Our platoon was fortunate that we drew a very pleasant Italian family and a comfortable dwelling. I have not seen any houses, as of yet, that are constructed of anything but stone but who are we to complain with a roof over our heads and three good meals a day. At night just before bedtime (usually around 9 PM) the family and our platoon, gather around the fire, chat and sip wine, which they always have plenty of.

Today, the senora of the house is stitching my blankets together in the form of a sleeping bag. She has offered to do it for nothing but I am willing to pay at least two dollars for the job. Some of the other fellows have had theirs done and I might say that she does a very nice job.

The other day we were given a real treat of a good shower and clean clothes. We stood in a long line outside of four or five tents awaiting our turn. When we got inside, we were handed two tags and a barracks bag. We stripped and put our clothes in the bag, attached a tag to it and kept the other. Then we went through the shower tent, a very systematic affair. There were perhaps seven or eight spouts in a row, all being used. You start at the first one and continue down the line as each one finishes at the end. All together you spend about ten or twelve minutes in the shower. When you are through some one grabs your tag and someone else tosses you a towel. Then your barracks bag is thrown at you. Before you know just what the system is, a fellow asks you for your pants and a clean pair is returned and so on, even the woolies. The last stage is the dressing compartment, a tent full of laughs as the clothes came in the two GI sizes, too large and too small. When we arrived at our area it was 7PM, long after chow, but provisions were made for us. I felt like a million dollars or something that stepped out of Rogers Pete (ha, ha).

Yesterday, Tiny, Eddie Myers, and I visited another family down the road several kilometers. I was astonished by their appearance. They looked so different from the ordinary Italian family that it was difficult for me to believe they were Italians. The girls were all fair heads except for one 13 year old who looked more like one of Mike Fallon's clan besides any Irishman I've seen in the States. The two oldest brothers are joining our outfit soon. We spent a pleasant afternoon with them making every effort to show our appreciation to them. Most of our efforts ended up in a laugh as no one understood.

As yet I am far behind in correspondence. Aunt Crucita wrote me a short letter and I was surprised to find that I hadn't written her in quite some time.

Tell Gram I received her card and note and to thank her very much for it. Tell her that I think she should forget about that letter incident with Nancy. I think she holds too much on her first impressions. Nelda Louise mentioned the subject to me also in a letter, recently so it's no longer a "hush, hush" matter. By the way she also stated that her marks have improved so that by September she can be initiated into Alpha Phi. Her finals came out better than expected. I feel confident now that she has made the "hump". She also told me about the sports activity at Syracuse but failed to mention Dolan as a basketball player. Is he? He certainly came through in the last game with Colgate.

It's time for hitting the hay.

Much love to you always,

Tink

February 6, 1945

Dear Clan, (letter to the Rautenberg family of Cleveland, Ohio)
    Yes, it is I-Hoople. I've finally settled myself enough so that I can write to the relatives.
    Received your Christmas package before I left the States. The socks are grand, especially in the mountains, where we are now. Thanks. Also received your letters recently. You all have certainly done a swell job of keeping me in contact with you. Sorry I am not able to correspond more frequently.

Before I explain your math problem, Ted III, (cousin) I would like to say that you are dealing with a genius in that field. My answer is this: your algebraic functions are correct but your problem becomes faulty when you divide by 0 or X-2. Since we know that X=2 then X-2=0. Therefore, dividing by 0 is impossible!! Have I given you a satisfactory answer?

My trip overseas proved very uninteresting until we passed through The Straits of Gibraltar. It is a very impressive rock but I was not quite as excited as I had anticipated. At Naples I caught a glimpse of what a bombed out city looks like. The waterfront especially, seemed to have taken most of the pounding. Since we passed through there at night, I was unable to see as much of the city as I would have liked. We spent some time traveling by rail, the GI deluxe method, by boxcar no less. The people have certainly seen enough destruction to last a life time. I saw a small boy, about ten years old, and a younger sister begging for food and money from the soldiers. Several of the fellows are of Italian descent and speak the native language fairly well. Through them, I was able to make out that the two children were begging for survival. It seems that their parents were killed in a bombing raid and they were living with a woman who was charging them room and board. Can you imagine the future of those kids?

Judging from your letter Johnnie, (Ted's cousin) you must have been a good boy last year because Santa Claus paid you a bountiful visit. Remember the walk we took while I was visiting you? Well, I had a swell time and hope that one day we'll be able to take another one, soon.

I hope that the trout up at Cranberry grow big and fat so that when we try our luck at the sport again, we won't have to pull out a ruler and measure them.

I'm winding up...I wish you all good health and a speedy recovery for you Aunt Crucita. Until I hear from you again,

Love "Hoople"

February 8,1945
(near the front in Italy)

Dear Mom,

I received 7 letters today after a long delay since the last one. Trying to answer everyone at one time is some problem. I have decided to write them in the order in which I think best.

The colored picture of you and Gram is swell but where did Gram purchase such a youthful rakish affair on her head?

Did I mention in my last letter that I was in the mountains and near the front? I suppose Mrs. McPherson keeps you well informed as to our outfit. I don't like the two of you knocking your heads together and comparing our notes. Maybe he shoots a better line than I do.

Yesterday the platoon went out on a patrol to one of our outposts. It was rough going as most of us have not done any activity of that kind for quite some time. The surroundings made me think of Camp Hale.

I better close for tonight as I go on guard duty shortly.

February 9, 1945
Write air-mail and V-mail. Air-mail preferably.

February 14, 1945
(on the front in the
shadow of Mt. Belvedere)

This is the first chance I have had to write since the 8th. We are on the front now experiencing many new and interesting things. Here on the outpost we have been shelled several times by the Germans. The house in which we are billeted is quite comfortable. The family that lived here has taken most of their household belongings with them, but we are making the best use of our domestic abilities to accommodate ourselves. Where I am sitting now, I am able to observe probable enemy strong points but as yet I have not seen a "Jerry". Every morning we are awakened by gunfire as our guns begin to shell the enemy. The Germans return a few rounds now and then but our concentration of fire is always superior in number. It's my turn for watch now so I'll close.

Love Always,

Tink

P.S. Please send a package of cookies, cake, and candy as soon as possible.

16 February 1945 – General Hays discusses his plans for the assault on Mt. Belvedere and its sister peak, Mt. Gorgolesca with a group of line soldiers from the 85th Regiment. This is unusual protocol for the commander of a whole division. Strategizing, face-to-face with the lead assault teams immediately creates a strong "esprit de corps" among the troops and a lasting loyalty to the General. He closes his speech saying, "You are the finest troops I've ever been associated with".

They are ready, willing and eager to fulfill their mission, planned back on January 8th by Fifth Army General Truscott. Still, they must wait until the advantage is gained on Riva Ridge.

Dear Gram H.

Yes, it is I, Ted, finally getting around to writing you. I did receive a card from the Readers' Digest before I left the States. It is amazing how they do fill so many subscriptions. The January issue arrived a week ago, as they still have my old address. How could I notify the Digest of my change of address, so that I could receive it on time? Thanks, Gram for sending it to me. It was the most useful of all my gifts.

Today we are resting after a short stay on the front. Most of us are dirty, unshaven, and fatigued. Nevertheless, we are in good spirits as we did have a comparatively easy time.

Several amusing incidents occurred which have aided my inexperience. The first night I was on patrol and while we passed through our post our scouts picked up another unit close by. The sign evidently, was not passed to the tail of the patrol where I was and consequently, I was fingering the end of my trigger not knowing they were friendly. As soon as the word came to move on, I realized it was a friendly unit.

For several nights our outpost was located in an old mountain farmhouse. Our lookouts were situated at windows on opposite sides of the house. Each man was assigned certain hours for watch.

Company I Rifleman on guard duty

Being unaccustomed to this type of warfare, we were all a little jittery. During his shift in the early morning, one fellow noticed a continuous rhythmic ticking and concluded it was a time bomb planted somewhere in the house. Immediately the whole household was astir and an investigation commenced. The alert was soon squelched, however, when we discovered water dripping from the roof onto the stone floor in one of the unoccupied rooms. The next evening after a quiet day, our cook was fetching water at the spring house, a few yards from the house, when the whine from a sniper's rifle was heard and the bullet whistled as it caromed off a rock. The following moment I saw a bent figure against the skyline racing through a hail of bullets to the door. For a while he was shaky but soon, we were all joking about it. We were greeted in the morning by our platoon leader in the same way.

That night one of our boys tripped a flare and it landed just outside the house on the poor farmer's haystack. In ten minutes, weeks and weeks of labor went up in flames and smoke. Of course, the Jerrys were most delighted by having a bull's eye and such an illuminated one at that. In a short while the distant sound of the German gun was heard and then the characteristic "swish, swish" of the shells in flight, and finally the explosions. Several were defective shells and did not explode. The rest were poorly aimed, indeed!! There was never a dull moment. Through censorship regulations, my experiences may not be so easily understood as I had wished, but I think you have been able to get the general drift.

I often think of those terrific Sunday night suppers with Hooples and olives galore. I wish that I could find something over here to take the place of the craving inside of me when Sunday evening comes around. I have yet to meet up with a family as true and loyal as the Hooples, and I am proud to be one of its members. Keep well Gram and say hello to the clan for me.

Much Love,
Ted

Riva Ridge, February 1945
Denver Public Library, 10th Mtn. Division Photographic Collections

18-19 February 1945 - On the evening of the 18th, 700 men of the 86th launch an assault on the 1700- to 2000-foot-high, Riva Ridge. They use five different routes that had been previously scouted and deemed possible. Two of those routes required fixed ropes ascending sheer rock walls in darkness. The surprise is complete and by daybreak they have gained the top at the cost of only one casualty. The German observation outposts along the ridge are well entrenched and fight back ferociously. It takes five days of reinforcements, supplies, medical evacuations, and bunker-to-bunker fighting to drive the Germans off. The initial success of the "Night Climb" sets off General Hays' plan to advance on Mt. Belvedere and Mt. Gorgolesca the following night.

BAR Team
Denver Public Library, 10th Mtn. Division Photographic Collections

19 February 1945 - At 11P.M., without artillery preparation, units from the 85th and 87th are ordered to fix bayonets and move out along the Line of Departure, heading up Mt. Belvedere. Their weapons are not loaded as a "grenades and bayonets only" order is given to avoid confusion in the darkness. Through the darkest hours, the troops advance in small groups through minefields and machine gun fire to get closer to the German positions. Finally, the lead groups are advised to load and fire at will. By dawn, after hours of heavy, close fighting, Belvedere is taken from the Germans and the troops turn their focus on the next objective, Mt. Gorgolesca. Other units of the 87th, including the 1st and 2nd Battalion are advancing on the heavily fortified small towns of Polla and Corona on the slopes of Belvedere. The night before, the 3rd Battalion, (Ted's), makes a grueling eight-mile march through ice and mud over a back trail to Vidiciatico to be held in reserve. They sustain their first combat casualty from a shell burst and their "Baptism under fire

"is now behind them. For the next six days, the 10th continues advancing north. They take mountain after mountain from the stunned, but still defiant, Germans, pushing their backs up against the wide-open Po Valley. The battles for Mt. Belvedere and the Mt. della Torracia cost the division 923 casualties: 192 KIA, 730 WIA and 1 POW. The heaviest fighting is yet to come.

27 February 1945 - Ted's 3rd Battalion, Company I, makes a probing maneuver to the northeast of Mt. della Torracia. It is their first sustained excursion into combat along the front lines and casualties are substantial. This kicks off the "March Offensive". The objective is another line of hills, five miles to the northeast, near the town of Castel d'Aiano. General Truscott believes this is the gateway through the German defenses to the Po Valley and ultimate victory.

3 March 1945 - Company I takes the lead on an incursion toward the mountain village of Pietra Colora, a known German command post with about 30 defenders. An Italian civilian points out a mine field in their path which they go around and approach the town from the rear of the defensive positions. Sniper fire and heavy artillery caused them to dig in; but by 5PM, along with their own artillery, the village was assaulted and taken. The American casualties are 2 dead, 6 wounded, and prisoners are taken.

Castel d'Aiano after the 87th drove the Germans out
Denver Public Library, 10th Mtn. Division Photographic Collections

5 March 1945 - The 87th captures the crossroads town of Castel d'Aiano, 15 miles north of Pietra Colora, as the 85th takes Mt. della Spe, a key ridge just to the east. This cuts the German line of communication and supply to the Po Valley. It is strongly contested by the Germans with counterattacks and heavy artillery bombardments over the next two weeks. The town of Castel d'Aiano is barely left standing. At the end of March through April 13th, this "March Offensive" costs the 10th Mountain Division 1012 casualties, 214 KIA, 794 WIA, and 4 POWS.

March 7, 1945
(near Castel d'Aiano)

Dear Folks,

I have received numerous letters from you and this is the first chance I have had to relax enough to write. We have certainly received our initiation of combat and from all reports and from my own conclusion we are darn good.

Bob Dudley captured one Kraut last evening and since Dud could speak German fairly well, he instructed the German, Walter Stroeber, to dig his foxhole and assist him with his pack. Since it was quite late in the evening, the prisoner was told to get into the foxhole with Dud and spend the night. This all seemed quite peculiar to Walter and to us also. Next morning, he was turned over to the POW section. He was 41 years old and came from Chemnitz, Saxony. I have many experiences to relate to you but at the moment I have not the time or the mental ease to write.

As of yet I have not received your package of Feb. 14. Anxiously awaiting its arrival. I'm sure I'll be able to make use of it if I have to pass it back and forth between our foxholes. Keep the letters coming. They are comparable to a steak dinner. If the butter and meat shortage get any worse, I'll send you some of my C and K rations. Ha, ha!

Love,

Ted

10-30 March 1945 - During these two and a half weeks of hill-to-hill and town-to-town fighting, the troops were rotated for three-day rests in safe towns well behind the front lines. There

was quite an exaggerated difference between the stress and fatigue of constant combat and the rest and relaxation of home-cooked meals, good Italian wine, and comfortable beds. For most, including, Ted and Bob Dudley, spirits were lifted. They returned to the front with new vigor and determination to end the war.

March 16, 1945
(from the front)

Dear Mom and Dad,

Like a furlough, our recent rest period of three days, offered so many things to do that I decided to postpone my correspondence until we returned to the front once again. And here we are witnessing another sunny Italian day. Frankly we all agree that we have been extremely fortunate in having continuous fair weather. Once we did experience cold snowy weather and that was just before the second push. We were dug in on the reverse slope of a long ridge waiting for zero hour. From our positions we could observe our objective very clearly. Once in a great while, with the aid of field glasses, we were able to see a German crawling from his hole for a breath of fresh air and returning as quickly as he had finished. It was just out of range of small arms, and besides any firing would have probably caused us more trouble than it was worth. We were content to observe and pick out their most likely positions which we would be storming soon. Zero hour was postponed for 36 hours which meant more sweating or nervous indigestion. During those hours we experienced heavy concentrations of mortar and artillery shells. Every time Jerry threw a barrage at us, we told him to dish out all he pleased because we were going to have a (censored) round barrage precede us. If you ever experienced an artillery duel that is a very comforting thought. We moved out sometime after the first elements. All along the way, I saw many unpleasant sights, in referring to our own men. But I saw many, many more pleasant sights of dead Germans and prisoners wandering back through our lines in groups of threes and fours. Some were wounded. All of them were frightened and as they passed, we jeered and shouted at them to increase their fear. This aids the interrogators' work. All positions were secured in the early afternoon. Our unit had another objective, which we would take if we reached our first one in good time and with low casualties. We reformed and moved down the forward slope of the ridge, headed for a town perhaps 1,000 yds. ahead. On our way down we were forced to pass through an open space for several hundred yards before we could reach any defilade. It was covered by a German machine gun.

The gun was firing from a great distance and therefore the bullets landed with great dispersion. This enabled us to pass on with little difficulty. We took the town shortly afterwards, capturing a number of prisoners, who offered only slight resistance. Following that we went on to take another ridge, which offered even lighter resistance. Apparently, we had them on the run.

I try to relate my experiences within the censorship bounds as truly as I have witnessed them. I don't believe in telling you all that I am seeing. I'll just leave it at that. My wish is that through me you are able to understand what is happening here on the front.

In my next letter, I hope to write about the rest area and how I met Tiny's uncle, who is an AMG Major here in Italy. Tiny's dad, by the way, graduated from Cornell in 1920, the same year you did from Syracuse, Dad. Perhaps you might recall the name.

Your Loving Son,

Ted

I'm very much interested in Med-o-lark (girls' camp). It sounds swell, an ideal set up. Glad to know this will be another successful camping season. I only wish I could be there to assist.

Please send food.

March 19, 1945
(from the front)

Dear Mom,

Our unit was fortunate in having been given a 3 day pass from the front lines to one of Italy's most famous summer resorts. The town was settled in a pleasant little valley surrounded by high peaks on all sides. It has been only slightly touched by war and it is as far as I can see the cleanest city we have been to.

Ted on 3-day pass with his platoon buddies
(Ted Reinero standing behind Ted)

As one passes along its streets, droves of GIs seem to appear from every house and side street, all walking in different directions as if they had some business to attend to. Actually, they were seeking the limited forms of entertainment offered by the Red Cross and the USO.

My great pleasure during my stay was a mineral bath accompanied by an Italian who served the private bathroom to the best of his ability. Of course, he was rather crude in his method of washing out the bath tub with a broom, but after living like a mole for several weeks it didn't bother me in the least.

A dinner, complete in three courses, could be purchased for only ten cents. The old army tradition of "sweating out the line" made it less appreciable.

I got a big kick out of the stage show when the chorus girls came out and did a smart dance routine. Some of them were very pretty, too!! Champagne was served at $3.25 a quart. Since I had never sampled any before, I could not tell if it was good, but the boys said it would cost at least $10 at home.

Well, we got a pretty good idea of what good ole fast civilian life used to be like. Rather than it being a "rest town" I think it was more like a "binge town" but the change was good for us all.

Have not received any packages so far, expecting one soon.

Love,

Ted

March 19, 1945
(from the front)

Dear Ruthie, (High School friend)

As secretary you are still doing a marvelous job. I was very pleased to receive your letter which took me totally by surprise. Your accounts of the basketball team and the game were so good that it was hard for me to believe that it was written by a woman. Of course, I realize how long you have been following up sports, but I just could not conceive such a perfect account by any woman.

Italy, as you know, is where I am fighting, in the most mountainous region to be found. As far as I can see, Italy is a war torn and devastated country and will only be self-supporting after years of reconstruction and revision. At one time, Italy must have been a very beautiful country although far behind us in modern civilization.

Perhaps you might enjoy reading some of my recent combat experiences. I will try not to pull any punches in my descriptions as it would spoil the true versions as I saw and experienced them.

Our first initiation into battle (Mt. Belvedere) came suddenly and in full force. We pulled into the area just after sundown after a long trek over the mountains. We dug in some 20 or 30 yards from a house along the more gentle slope of the mountain. This was the most likely approach for the enemy. Darkness is generally one of our best friends but during this incident it wasn't. It must have been 5 AM after the moon had set. We were half asleep in our foxholes when I heard voices coming from the corner of the house. At first, none of us paid any attention to the matter. Then someone shouted "Halt!" and several figures started to run. Rifle fire opened up and I saw two or three drop. The rest got away. Later we found out they had circled back around to a house about 30 yards in front of us. Twenty minutes passed and then all hell broke loose. The Germans were firing from houses with every kind of weapon imaginable except artillery. Apparently, they were determined to get us as we noticed a patrol on our flank up the ridge. Luckily one of our units was up there and the count was 16 dead. Back in our position we could count at least 7 Jerrys lying in the snow in front on the side and even among us. Blood smeared bodies and groaning men was a sickening sight at that moment, for we had a lull in the firing to observe. One of our men took advantage of the opportunity and crawled out to the first building using a hedgerow for cover. He shouted for the Germans to surrender. At first, they came out in twos and threes and later in eights and tens. The final count was 37 captured and 9 dead Jerrys.

After we had captured a long ridge later, we had the alternative of taking a town in the valley below or digging in on the ridge. With that aggressive spirit prevailing, down we went. About half way we had to cross an open space affording no cover whatsoever. At this point we were fired on by a German machine gun. Luckily it was firing from a great distance and we advanced with no casualties. It seemed like another "problem" (training exercise) we were running back in the States. Later I had thought over what had happened with a little different aspect. We took the town quickly, capturing only a few Jerries. That night we were digging in along the roadside, just inside the town limits when two figures made their way toward us. Since there had been quite a number of our boys passing along the road, we paid no attention and continued digging. They passed us without causing any suspicion. We discovered the next morning that two armed Germans were captured inside our defense ring. How about that?

Running out of paper, Ruthie, Give my best to Gus and Your family.

Best regards from the old Treasurer and good friend, Ted

19-20 March 1945 - After writing the two preceding letters during the day of March 19th, Ted's Company I was selected to conduct a night patrol that evening. Being a BAR man (30 caliber light machine gunner), it is almost certain that he was among the 30 men chosen along with his older pal, Bob Dudley. In the following letter, Bob Dudley's wife, Helen, all but confirms this. The mission was to take a small group of farm houses, in a village where enemy activity had been observed. They were to capture as many prisoners as possible for interrogation purposes. They crossed a mine field in the moonlight that had been previously scouted and mapped out for them. As they held their undetected position on the outskirts of the small village, an artillery barrage was called in around 3 AM. Minutes after the barrage ended, they stormed the largest farmhouse and ushered out 23 German prisoners who had been taking cover in the cellar.

10th Mountain taking German prisoners
Denver Public Library, 10th Mtn. Division Photographic Collections

They got what they came for and efficiently left, just 15 minutes after the barrage had ended with even more prisoners. With the high prisoner count and no casualties, it has been cited as one of the most successfully conducted patrols ever sent out in the Italian Theater.

Bob Dudley and Ted on a 4-day pass from the front

A letter from Mrs. Helen Dudley to Nelda Hoople:

Topsham, Maine
March 25, 1945

Dear Mrs. Hoople,

It has been some time since I received your letter. I meant to answer it before but first I was sick in bed for nearly two weeks with a miserable cold. Then Jane had bronchitis and she was in in bed two weeks too. However, we are all over our spring colds now and able to enjoy the sunshine. The children are busy with marbles, jump ropes, and getting in puddles of water.

I had a long letter from Robert over a week ago telling me about the part he took in the battle on Mt. Belvedere. He killed at least two Germans and captured 9 or 10. The patrol he was with killed 7 that day and captured about 50 or so. Bob told about Ted and himself taking 23 prisoners and then Bob went back into the cellar and captured 9 more and 3 machine guns. Later he found another German hiding in a cabinet. Anyway, Bob wrote for me to tell you that your Ted came through the battle of Belvedere safely. Bob's name was in the paper telling about his part in the battle. He is going to receive a citation I believe. I'm very proud of him. Since then, they have been in another battle and I'm waiting to hear how he got through the second one. So many boys from northern New England have been casualties I hardly dare look at the newspaper each morning.

It certainly is a tough job they have to do there in Italy. I spend half my time cutting Italian communiques out of the papers or listening to news broadcasts hoping to hear something about Italy. I sure hope your Ted and my Bob, and Eddie and Tiny get through it alright. But for the children's' sake I can't let myself get glum or worried. I think of you lots and hope I can meet you sometime.

Sincerely,
Helen Dudley

March 31, 1945
(10th Mountain Division Rest Center
behind the lines)

Dear Mom and Dad,

Hurray!! The package, which I have been expecting for so long, has arrived with all its contents as you told me. The football is really something to have these days. As for Pinkie's knife, it is exactly what I had wished for. When Dud took a look at it, he remarked, "Whoever sent this really had some sense because it is oiled thoroughly". I told him, "That's putting it mildly" but I'm afraid I'm the only one who could appreciate the jest.

184

At the present moment I am sitting on a soft bed in a hotel room at our Division rest center. Three from our unit drew four day passes and "yours truly" made the team. I brought another letter which I had written several days before and I left it in the room here. That's right it's gone now. I presume the chambermaid (we have them) thought it was just another piece of paper and dropped it in the stove (we have them too). I had my picture taken yesterday. It's going to be a honey. I won't tell you any more about it but I'll let you see for yourselves.

There are many different forms of entertainment here; movies, USO shows, Red Cross Clubs, Dances, jam sessions and excellent meals. For breakfast this morning we had tomato juice, cereal, scrambled eggs and toast, coffee and oranges. They certainly try to make you as comfortable as possible. Although last night the bed was too soft and I woke up with a kink in my back this morning.

Tomorrow is Easter Sunday. I shall spend the day in much more comfort than last Easter. I remember then, when I awoke, it was snowing very hard and everyone was miserably wet and cold. Quite a difference this year and even the news brightens the atmosphere.

I saw Russell Minot the other day. He told me his wife lost her 2nd child about a month ago. I didn't bother to press him for further details so we just chatted for a few minutes and parted. He's a good fellow, a little hard to know at first, though.

Things have quieted down so much that any real news is hard to scrape up. Most of the boys are in good spirits as the end of the European War draws closer. Occasionally a deserter comes across the line. They are not the true-blue Germans but Yugoslavs who have been forced to fight. One showed us his daily ration which consisted of two small pieces of cruddy cheese and a piece of bread. The longer the Germans continue to resist, the angrier the GIs get. Who knows, maybe by the time you receive this letter the show will be over. Happy Easter to you.

Love,

Ted

Ted sporting a Van Dyke

April 6, 1945
(back at the front)

Dear Mom and Dad,

Enclosed are the pictures I had taken just before Easter. The "Van Dyke" and the moustache are a novelty which a lot of us have tried. Some boys are successful, others are just kidding themselves. When you look at the picture, I can imagine any number of exclamations you might make. I am letting it grow either until the war is over or I am ordered to shave it off.

I dug up a German Schu Mine the other day, which I hope to send home one of these days. When cleaned up and varnished it will make a swell souvenir, cigarette box, or some other ornament for the mantel or the tea stand. It's not every day that one gets to pick up a souvenir like that but someone found a minefield and a number of us were chosen to dig them up. The main purpose was that we learn to disarm them and understand the functioning. Perhaps by a diagram, I can give you an idea of how it works.

to dig them up. The main purpose was that we learn how to disarm them and understand the functioning. Perhaps by a diagram I can give you an idea of how it works.

Side View   SCHU MINE   Front View

Butterfly
Pin

Top Open View

2-6 lb Pressure & Butterfly
Pin is released

Igniter   ← 1/2 lb Dynamite

Firing Pin &
Compressed Spg.

Booster or
Blasting Cap

In The Ground

Probing

Sod Over
Top

and they are all sprawled out on the ground taking in a hot sun bath on a slope in the Appenines under the famous warm Italian sun.

Ted's diagram of a German Shu Mine from his letter home

188

Recovered German Schu Mine with applied Edelweiss patch and decoration

Dud, Tiny, and the boys are all sprawled out on the ground taking in a hot sun bath on a slope in the Apennines, under the famous warm Italian sun.

Things I speak of, as action, have been quiet the past few days. That is good news which continues and raises our spirits to no end. We toss the football around quite a bit but because there are so many hills and uneven ground, our war cry is "On to the Po where we can play a real game!"

I'm very pleased with the way the registrations are coming in as far as the girls' camp. Aunt Ruth and Evelyn Derry are the best to be had in that field. I hope it will be a good summer for you. At least you have a great start. Keep me posted on the details as I feel like I'm right there with you, if only in spirit.

Love Always,

Ted

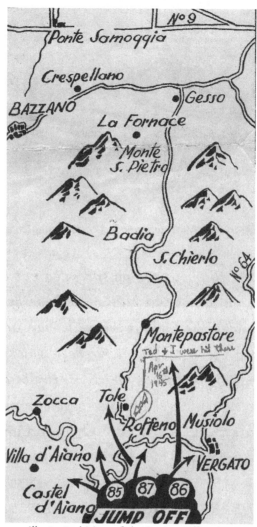

Illustrated Map of the Spring Offensive
Blizzard Magazine, May 22, 1945, Vol. 4

14 April 1945 - The Spring Offensive begins. The 10th Mountain is once again the tip of the spear with the three battalions being skillfully orchestrated through the mountains and villages by the high command, backed up by their mobile light artillery. The 87th pushes northward from Castel d'Aiano towards the town of Torre lussi.

The Remnants of Torre Iussi after the 87th regiment pushed through
Denver Public Library, 10th Mtn. Division Photographic Collections

They are the middle regiment of the three-pronged advance. They plow ahead, platoon by platoon, suffering staggering losses. They leapfrog each other and secure every bit of ground along the way. House-to-house fighting and German bunker assaults over rough terrain are the order of the day. German artillery bombardment is almost constant and very costly. Prisoners are taken, but many who resist are not. As they approach the Town of Torre Iussi, Company I is in the lead. They become pinned down by 18 Germans with machine guns on the slopes of the hill above the town. Two BAR teams from the second platoon get positioned and neutralize the machine guns. They continue to move forward until ordered to halt at midnight on the south slope of Mt. Croce and dig in. The past 24 hours account for the bloodiest day on the field of battle for the 10th Mountain Division.

The open ground where Sgt. Reinero and PFC Hoople were wounded
with Mt. Mosca in the background
Davide Demaria, 2020

16 April 1945 - at dawn Company I moved cautiously up the slope of Mt. Croce above the village of Tole' and attempt to dig into the rocky ground below the summit. Soon, German sniper fire was directed at them. Shortly, a heavy, concentrated barrage blanketed the company area, indicating an artillery spotter had them sighted in. Instantly, one man was killed and three seriously wounded. Immediate action was needed to neutralize the spotter and the snipers. Sergeant Ted Reinero along with his BAR man, Ted Hoople, sprinted forward into the open field to get a closer view of the German positions and mount an attempt to take them out. The bursting shells were too numerous and they were both hit. When shells hit the ground, they explode upwards causing severe body wounds. A hot piece of shrapnel grazed PFC Hoople's chest and tore up and into his left triceps. The pocket bible (from his Grandmother)

and fork and spoon set he carried in his left breast pocket were burned and badly damaged.

The shrapnel just missed his heart by inches. Sergeant Reinero was more severely wounded and had to be helped back to their lines. For this effort, PFC Hoople was given a citation and awarded the Bronze Star.

Shortly after that, the Company Commander, Captain Adrian Riordan, moved his troops up the hill to the higher ground but were pinned down by automatic weapons fire while the barrage continued. He placed machine gun units on the right flank and drove the Germans back into the morning fog. They routed five more Germans out of the dugout at the top. It was found to be the artillery observation post that had probably zeroed in on them. They destroyed the communications equipment and the artillery barrage ceased. Company I moved on to support the action taking place on Mt. Mosca. Sergeant Reinero and PFC Hoople were taken back to a field hospital. As Company I was heading toward Mt. Mosca, more of the same type of action was taking place.

This eyewitness account, by "Pete" Petersen Platoon Leader, Company I, 87th, was recorded in "Packs On" by A. B. Feurer, Stackpole Books 2004. "I was given the mission of seizing Mt. Mosca and hill 779 by Captain Riordan. The hill rose about 500 feet and extended about 1000 feet along its base. As we spread out and advanced toward our objective, several men on the left of the line had to cross an open area. The rest of the platoon received some cover from a wooded area and a gully. Suddenly, as we moved forward, an enemy sniper began firing at the unprotected men. John Spreng was shot. Barton Morrison, the platoon medic, hurried to his aid but was also struck down. The sniper kept shooting at the two fallen soldiers, even though the Red Cross on the medic's helmet was clearly visible. Willard Nichols and I, using the gully for cover, were able to sneak within several yards of them, but they appeared dead and didn't respond when I called out to them... When the bodies were recovered, they had multiple gunshot wounds. Morrison had been shot more than twenty times... Just before dusk I saw Orville Cockrill, armed with a BAR, herding the captured sniper to the rear. I remarked to Cockrill that this was the person who killed Morrison and Spreng. Minutes later a shot rang out near our command post. When asked what happened, Cockrill replied that his prisoner had tried to escape. The sniper's body was found in a ditch alongside the road."

The three days of the Spring Offensive were the costliest of the 10th Italian campaign. The Division suffered 1336 casualties: 286 KIA, 1047 WIA, and 3 POWs. The German line had finally been broken through. They began a disorganized retreat from their mountain peaks down the northern slopes of the Apennines into the Po Valley.

12   WM 45   42 GOVT WUX WASHINGTON DC   9 35 A MAY 4

HOWARD C HOOPLE

65 LEWIS RD BELMONT MASS

THE SECRETARY OF WAR DESIRES ME TO EXPRESS HIS DEEP REGRET THAT YOUR
SON PFC. HOOPLE, THEODORE G. WAS SLIGHTLY WOUNDED IN ITALY 16 APRIL, 45.
CONTINUE TO ADDRESS MAIL TO HIM AS FORMERLY OR UNTIL NEW ADDRESS IS RE-
CEIVED FROM HIM.

          J A ULIO THE ADJUTANT GENERAL

                              10.12 A

Telegram to Ted's father, Howard, informing him of Ted's injury

April 23, 1945
(from U.S. Army 20 General Hospital,
Pistoia, Italy)

Dear Folks,

I am enjoying not all, but many of the comforts of
home. Sleeping in sheets, having breakfast served to me
in bed etc. etc. Since I am progressing rapidly back to my
normal self, special attention and service has become
more limited. I am under the assumption that you have
received notice of my being wounded in the left arm, on
the 16th, by shrapnel. Except for the immobilization of
my arm, I feel great and "raring to go".

Please explain to the relatives it is rather difficult for one to write, as you remember, I am left-handed. Tiny and Dud are still hammering away at the Jerries. One last report was that Dud bagged five the other day.

Love,
Ted

Ted receives the Purple Heart for being wounded in battle

2 May 1945 - the German Army in Italy surrenders. In northern Europe, the Germans fight on.

May 2, 1945
(U.S. Army 12 General Hospital,
Livorno, Italy)

Dear Mom and Dad,

As I start this letter I am sitting beside the radio in the hospital listening to the report of the surrender, unconditionally, by the German command of all forces in the Mediterranean Theater, to the Allies. For a group of supposedly wounded men in this ward, I am surprised at the immediate rejoicing. You can't imagine how really wonderful the news seems to us. Although the war continues, the final struggle in Italy is over, and that is something!!! It can be done.

I wish I could tell you where I am and describe some of the scenery but I'll save that until I am home. I am in excellent spirits having been fed well and treated with the best possible care. One of my most treasured comforts in an inner spring mattress only a few of the most privileged characters are allowed. I expect to be kicked out any moment. I really miss your letters. The reason for delay is obvious but my patience is limited. I probably have a dozen letters and packages waiting for me now.

The latest report from the front is that Dud is doing a tremendous job. He is always out in front taking unheard of risks and knocking off German snipers. At one place he forced a machine gun squad to surrender. As a combat soldier he is tops. It is mostly due to his training at Norwich University. Tiny sprained his ankle the other day. He is so darn big (6'7" and 253 lbs.) but he is as good as any of the rest when the going gets rough. I actually wish I could be up there with the boys right now. A few days of relaxation back here is wonderful but I am getting very restless. This is no place for me when I feel that good. Does it sound like I'm bucking for a section VIII?

How is camp coming along? Gee, I'll bet you'll have a terrific summer. As for Med-o-Lark, I'm all for it. I would like to hear more about it in detail if you have a few spare moments.

I have met a fellow, who like myself, is very much interested in the outdoors especially trout fishing. We spend a great deal of time swapping stories. His generally top mine when it comes to size. You guessed it. He comes from the Northwest. Someday I plan to try my Eastern skills on a few of those streams and lakes where such fabulous stories originate.

One more mentioning of the war before I close. I respect the great courage it took for our men to begin and end this long campaign in the Mediterranean. I know now how they felt sometimes when it dragged on and on and the going was tough. My hat's off to them, from a rookie.

Love always,
Ted

7 May 1945: Germany surrenders

Dear Mom and Dad,

The final end came not as a surprise but as an anticlimax over here. Last night the walking patients and the hospital personnel gathered around a huge bonfire to celebrate the end of Nazism. The swastika was suspended from a pole over the fire. We watched it burn away and with it all of our bad memories and long suffering under its influence (for good, we hope!). We sang several songs; The Star-Spangled Banner, Home on the Range, etc. The Red Cross served coffee and doughnuts, but the crowd was dull, no life to it, so I returned to the ward.

My arm is nearly healed by now. I expect to return to duty in the next few days. It's still a tender spot and I should imagine that it will take a couple of weeks before the stiffness leaves.

I presume that you have heard of the point system of discharging European Vets? 85 points allows a man to be discharged. I am just 39 points short with a total of 46. So, it definitely looks like a lot of fighting ahead for me (the 10th was secretly scheduled for the invasion of Japan in November). I hope we will make the States before going to C.B.I (China, Burma, India aka the Pacific Theater). There has been a lot of talk and rumors. Certainly, one must be true as they cover a very wide variety.

I haven't heard from anyone from the company except those I meet down here. I'm anxious to get back to find out what the score is.

I have seen a number of movies lately but none of them have been worth it. It was just something to take your mind off of other things. One USO troupe made a big hit with us "dog faces". Strange as it may sound it was not a group of pretty chorus girls with terrific shapes. It was a Negro religious choir which sang many high classed spirituals. Everyone in the choir was able to solo but only a few did and were they good.

The nurses and doctors continue to give me a hard time about my Van Dyke. That one time on the operating table I was sure it was going. The doctor and nurse looked down at me with a gleam in their eyes, which I was sure spelled destruction for my whiskers.

Lying around for a month has sure made a softy out of me. I finally did get kicked off that inner spring mattress. I've gained weight and now I'm up to 182. I'm certainly making up for lost time when it comes to food. I have a friend in the yellow jaundice ward. I go over there and drink milk and pineapple juice and eat jam sandwiches with him when I'm not down at the mess hall. Here's hoping.   Love, Ted

Dear Mom,

Today being Mothers' Day I felt that at least I should drop you a line. My financial status is so crippled I have been forced to borrow a few dollars in order to obtain my rations. I have not been paid since March 2nd so you can imagine what a wad I have coming.

I am planning on going to church this morning which is not a regular habit with me over here. This morning is a special occasion as it has been proclaimed a day for prayer and thanksgiving. I can see no better way to express my feelings for the boys we left behind. Through their sacrifice we survived.

I suppose you're getting "dolled up" for church yourself. With the pay I have coming we could go to the finest restaurant in Boston. $10 a plate wouldn't be good enough. Yeah, I'm out to "blow my wad" today. Getting back to reality now. Here at the hospital the Red Cross has arranged for some movies tonight and the hospital baseball team plays this afternoon so I have a very full schedule ahead.

I received a letter from you yesterday acknowledging that I was wounded but the wound is in the left arm, not the leg as you stated. Tomorrow I plan to rejoin the outfit. They are quite a ways north of here. It will probably take several days before I catch up with them.

At the present time I am sunning myself on a beach overlooking the ocean. It is warm enough to go swimming. I have been soaking up the sun for several days now but I can never tan properly. Eventually I end up with a reddish-brown color as you know.

Perhaps I can explain why Howard's patch is embarrassing to him. Perhaps it was one of those "dog face" infantry men who sneered. I will try to give you an idea why. First, I believe he is jealous of Howie's position (Medical Corps officer) which is ideal you must admit. After the war he is set with hardly any expense on his part. Secondly, a "dog face" is cocky. He has to be because he feels that his position is inferior and without distinction. This is entirely untrue but nevertheless he feels that way.

Well, time for me to be on my way to church soon so I will close shortly.

Yesterday I got hold of a glove and a ball and tried loosening my arm gradually. The stiffness is still there but, in a few days, it should work out. I am conscious of it all the time and keep moving it back and forth. In a few days you would never be able to tell I was hit.

I expect to hear from you again today as you said you were going to write more frequently.

Until later, Love, Ted

20 May 1945 - The 10th moves to Udine in northeastern Italy near Trieste. Its mission is to join with troops of the British 8th Army to prevent renegade and communist Yugoslavian troops from expanding westward into Italian territory.

May 23rd, 1945

(north of Trieste)

Dear Folks,

I have been returned to my old stomping grounds once more. It seems good to see the boys again although there are many new faces which remind me of the early days of my army career. Tiny, Dud, and Eddie are all in good health so you can see that we as a group have been tremendously fortunate.

Once again mountains surround our camp. From the windows in this house I am able to see another country of Europe.

Yesterday I went fishing in one of the most ideal mountain streams I have yet seen. The fishing is poor at this time of year as the fish have just spawned and they are eating their newborn. I propositioned a few natives for some flies and hooks. My efforts were not in vain as I did manage to snag two trout. One was about 12 inches and one was about 7. The larger one was about the same as our American Rainbow, except for the purple tint. The other resembled our Eastern Speckled Trout with a more silvery complexion. Both were excellent eating. My time, as you can see, is limited for this type of recreation. During the existing tense situation, I will probably have even less time. Also, we are moving around a lot.

I've been exercising my arm regularly; tossing the football and baseball around, trying to loosen the muscles. There have been no after effects except a slight numbness below the wound which does not bother me in the least.

The people in these hamlets do not seem as friendly to us as others we have come in contact with. I believe our warm cheerfulness and our ever-prevalent characteristic of generosity is slowly destroying the coolness of their attitudes.

At the present time there is a heated discussion on world affairs. Who are the best fighters, who are the greatest and mightiest, etc. A great deal of credit is being given to the British as fighters. We have discussed El Alamein, Dunkirk, the Battle of Britain, etc. Most everyone agrees that the "Limeys" deserve a great deal of credit in enabling us to end the war. The argument has been called off for 18 minutes so that we can continue letter writing. Tiny has been defending the Americans while Dud and I are siding with the British. It has really developed into a heated argument so we have decided to cool off for a moment. The uncertainty of our future is a continual topic for discussion. The most ardent desire of all is that we return to the States for a furlough before continuing on. Dud and I got some eggs from a farmer the other day. For once, we enjoyed them as one does back home. Powdered eggs have become as monotonous as steak did back in Texas. When the Black Market deal in France blew up, we were all happy to read the sentences passed on the gangsters. When you're on the front, risking your lives and the food lines are cut, you curse the bums that are profiting from the war. Well here's hoping again.

Love,

Ted

5 PM.

Censorship has just been lifted. First of all, we are approximately 32 miles north of Trieste close to the Yugoslav border sweating out the Tito situation. Most of us here feel that he is entitled to the darn port but for once our State Department has decided to get tough with these little "Big Shots". The situation is difficult for us because if it becomes serious, we do not know quite what to shoot at. Women walk around packing sub-machine guns. Even old men and young boys are difficult to distinguish from the Italians. Then there are the Italian partisans who think that they should have the port. Yes, the situation is all a snafu.

I was hit near Tole, Italy, just a few miles short of the Po Valley west of Bologna. I was in the 20th General

Hospital at Pistoia and then transferred to the 12ᵗʰ General at Leghorn (Livorno).

Probably you know we landed in Naples and on our way up we stopped in Pisa and visited the Leaning Tower.

Rumors flash around since the censorship has been lifted, that we will remain here for several months. When censorship starts again it will probably indicate movement and we hope that it will be to the States.

We lost during the push over half the platoon—27 men and quite a number of those killed.

Compared to other outfits we came out of it very well. Write with any questions you have soon.

May 23, 1945
(north of Trieste)

Dear Gene, (Cousin Gene Carver)

Well how's the boy? Say thanks a million for writing me that letter. I certainly enjoy hearing from all the relatives but I can't expect to hear from them unless I write. I owe your sister one now. If you see her, tell her it's not that I don't like her anymore but that I hope she's lost weight worrying about me (ha, ha).

With the war being over now, you would think that we have nothing to do around here. Well, you know the Army, and with the tense international affair, which arose out of the capture of Trieste by the Italian partisans and the Yugoslavs led by Tito, Tito seems to think that he should have the port as do the Italian partisans. But we say no. Let the San Francisco Conference settle the question among the Allied Nations. It so happens that our division (10th Mountain) has been one of the fortunate ones to take care of the situation in case the fireworks start. The trouble is that it is difficult to discern who's who. Women walk around packing sub-machine guns. Even young kids are packing pistols. It now appears from the latest reports that the verbal conflict will be sufficient. Let's hope so.

Yesterday I managed to slip away just about dusk with a homemade fly rod, a spool of string, and a homemade fly. The river (perhaps you can locate it on the map) is approximately 30 miles north northeast of Bologna. Udine, another city, lies 20 miles to the south. This river is an ideal mountain trout stream with beautiful clear water which has carved deep pools under rocks that line the banks. During this month the fish are spawning and they feed on their young so you can imagine my luck being slim. I did manage to catch two. One 13 inch and one 8 inch.

(Author's Note: this proves Ted is a "true, blue" Isaack Walton devotee as both fish have already grown an inch since the previous letter that day).

The larger one resembled the American Rainbow, the other the Eastern Brook trout with a more silvery color. Perhaps in a few weeks my luck will change. I know they're in there because I could see them. Let me tell you it was a great thrill to go up there because it reminded me of past experiences at Cranberry Lake.

Well, I was all set for a rating as a Sgt. but when I got hit a replacement got the spot. That's the way my luck runs. I guess I'm in a good position where I am, without extra responsibilities and having to look after anyone.

It looks like we will stay here for some time as they have lifted the censorship regulations and that means no troop movements. I would just as soon sweat it out right here. One war is enough for me, but we have to be ready at a moment's call. Thanks again Gene. Let's hear from you again.

Good Luck. Love, Ted

May 25, 1945
(north of Trieste)

Dear Mom,

Here is the blow by blow description of the final push of the 10th Mountain Division. This ought to be the most important page in your scrapbook. I wish that I could send you some pictures which were taken while we've been over here. There is one fellow here, my ex squad leader, Sergeant Ted Reinero of Merced, California, who is one of the finest men I have ever known. He and I were hit together on the ridge overlooking Tole, which I have marked on the map as you can see.

There is still no indication of our moving out. In fact, we built a baseball diamond yesterday. Dud and I cut the grass, entirely by ourselves, some 250 feet square. We borrowed one of the farmer's scythes. Dud says I am a born farmer. I, for the sake of argument, say that city life is the place for me.

This is just a short note with a lot of reading material so read it and enjoy yourself.

Love,

Tink

June 11, 1945

(Tarvisio)

Dear Mom and Dad,

I presume by now you have completed your business in the city and are preparing to leave for camp. It was wonderful news to know that Medomak is on its way to the best year in its history. Perhaps Med-o-lark can boast a proud record like Medomak in a few years. I wish I could be up there. At least I could act as a Teddy Coombs during the summer months.

Perhaps you have heard that the Trieste situation has cleared without incident and now we are really sweating out our next move. Some predict a five month stay in Austria as occupational troops before coming home, on our way to the Pacific.

At the present our training consists of the following, strictly a GI schedule:

Revelie-0600

Mess-0700

Exercise-0800

Close order drill-0900
Orientation-1100
Mess-1200
Organized sports-1:00
Retreat-5:30
Mess- 5:45

During the morning our schedule varies. Sometimes instead of following the list we take off to a nearby mountain. We climb until about 11:00 AM and then whether or not we reach the top (we usually do) we descend and return for lunch. At a glance this would appear to be a very enjoyable period in our army career but being isolated for so long in these mountains among people who survive by the hand and hoe tends to throw a guy off balance.

We've played baseball, football, and even track but in the army, sports are in a class by themselves. Often you find "Joe or Willie" playing second base when he has never played the sport before. The army insists that he put on a glove and stand 10 feet to the right of the bag. It's hard to stir up any enthusiasm this way.

Another fellow and I tied a couple of flies the other day and went fishing after supper that evening. This time our luck wasn't as good as the last time. We did hook one about 8 inches long. I cut a pole from a scrub bush. It was about an inch in diameter and approximately 9 feet long. When I hooked the trout, I nearly snapped the leader and fly because I couldn't feel the fish with that heavy rod. When I saw that I did have him hooked, I tried to play him but it was no use. I just hauled him in with the old "Peavine (Creek) horseplay". If I knew we were going to be here any length of time, I would ask for some equipment like leader, flies, and line. I shall leave it up to your discretion.

How is Med-o-lark coming along? Keep me posted on the latest news.

Until later

Love, Ted

June 23, 1945
(Tarvisio)

Dear Mom and Dad,

The situation here, concerning our future as a division has cleared somewhat. Starting July 2nd everyone is required to take 3 subjects in the army's new educational program for occupational forces. This does not mean that we are definitely occupational forces, but it does imply we will be in Europe for at least three months, starting July 1st. In this set up the most points I can scrape up will be 58 which is just the reverse of 85. Have you heard of any late rumors of the point system being lowered?

At the present time and during the next 8 weeks I am acting as a rock climbing and mountaineering instructor. The location of this school is east of Tarvisio on the borders of Yugoslavia and Austria. The partly snow covered, rugged peaks, remind me of Colorado's Rockies. We are about 60 miles from our base camp south of Caporetto. It is still undecided as to whether the school will remain open while the educational program is going. I hope it does not interfere as we are bivouacked beside a small spring fed pond full of large German Brown Trout. The water is so clear that it is very difficult to catch them without the proper equipment. So far, I have managed to catch only three.

You would be surprised at the number of people who are interested in mountains. Friday night we took a trip up to a small cabin near the timberline (6,000 to 7,000 feet altitude). While we were cooking supper a group of three came trudging up the path. An elderly man, his son and daughter, all carrying packs suited to their size. Eddie Myers, the fellow from Springfield, can speak German quite fluently. So, with his interpreting we managed to have quite an enjoyable conversation over a cup of coffee we made. The father was in the last war and also an Alpinie (guide) in this one. His daughter is 20 and is she nice! Wow. She was born in Munich and later moved to Tarvisio. At the present time she is studying at Trieste. The ole man went out and cut a number of boughs so we gathered they were planning to stay with us for the night as we were. Ed and I crawled into our sleeping bags around the fire and gave them the use of the cabin. Fortunately, it did not rain. Sometime during the night, Ed woke up and whispered, "Get your gun, I think we are going to have some wild goat meat! I looked to where he was pointing and I saw two phosphorescent eyes staring at us. Suddenly the eyes crossed! It was only a pair of fire flies. I laughed for 5 minutes over that one. At 5 AM the following morning the other party had breakfast and departed for the 8.800 foot summit. Ed and I slept on. Later in the day we traveled east to the borderline. It was noon when we reached it as the climb was quite steep. We straddled the rock marker and practiced yodeling. Presently a flock of sheep wandered our way. When they discovered we were "phonies" they gave us the "ba-aaa ba" and took off. We did not see any wild game probably because we had our guns and we were after it. An hour later we were back at the cabin packing up to return and wash up, change our clothes and go to the Saturday night dance in the village. It is just 2 ½ miles down the Tarvisio road.

I should say Happy Birthday Mom, a little late as usual. I'll try and find some Edelweiss and send it to you as compensation.

Lovingly,

Ted

You asked about Ganz. Do not know of him. Received your letter while at the 12th Gen. Hospl. He was at 70th?

P.S. Special for Pop. I believe you asked for the details of the treatment I received when I was hit:

On the 16th of April we were in the lead squad of the Company moving laterally along a ridge above Tole'.

The remains of Tole, Italy, April 15, 1945 with the Po Valley in the background
Denver Public Library, 10th Mtn. Division Photographic Collections

We stopped for a brief moment. During that time, we were to dig in on the reverse slope to avoid artillery, which was coming in heavier concentration than usual. We figured that someone had good observation. Ted Reinero, the Squad leader, asked for covering fire from the BAR, my gun, while he investigated the slope ahead. In order for me to cover him properly, I had to go along with him. We heard the Germans talking 150 yards up ahead. We shouted for them to surrender but they didn't see it our way. One got out of the bunker and ran. We fired but it was difficult to see whether we got him or not. Suddenly, SWISH... BOOM!!! And that was that. We were both hit but able to make it back together. The medics were busy at that time with the more seriously wounded and therefore some squad members helped us out. First, they sprinkled sulfa powder on the arm from the first aid packet each man carries. Then they bandaged my arm. Ted Reinero's artery was severed. By the time the boys ripped off his shirtsleeve, at least a cup of blood had spurted out. Tourniquets were used on both of us before anything else was done. "Stop the bleeding, first" had always been stressed in our training. They gave Ted a shot of morphine and I helped him back to the aid station. At the aid station they were handling cases as fast as they came in, but later, only the more serious cases were handled first. We were given a new change of bandages there while we waited for transportation to a collecting center. Six hours later we arrived at the collection center quite weary, as we had gone the past two days without sleep. We were given some coffee there while waiting for transportation to an evacuation hospital. It was 9:30 when we arrived at the hospital. The more serious cases that needed plasma transfusions were treated first. We were given tetanus and penicillin shots while our records were being processed. A half hour later we boarded another ambulance for the 70th General Hospital. We arrived there at 2AM about 80 or 90 miles from the front. We were given a sedative after x-rays and records were taken. At 4 AM we were operated on. The first thing they did was clean the wound out. By the following afternoon we were taking penicillin every three hours. Four days later we were sewed up and 7 days later the sutures were taken out. I was transferred to the 12th General Hospital for recuperation before returning to the outfit.

June 28, 1945
(Tarvisio)

Dear Mom and Dad,

Rock climbing in the Alps has been quite a novelty for me. We have had platoons up here for the past 3 weeks. By this time, I feel quite capable of instructing the fundamentals of rock climbing and mountaineering. Our schedule runs something like this: Monday we instruct a few basic fundamentals in mountaineering such as the "rest step", breathing, making use of the many opportunities which nature affords, and the appreciation of wildlife and scenery. We do not present it to them as though it were an important part of the training so that they don't feel forced to learn. Rather than that, we work it in during the week, a little here and a little there. Of course, there are always a few who are "goldbricks" and refuse to cooperate. But as a whole, the various groups have grasped the spirit of camping and the out of doors. Tuesday we spend entirely up on the rocks; teaching the various hand and footholds. We practice free climbing on the gentle rock slopes in order that the men gain confidence in themselves. Wednesday, we present a new phase in rock work. That is descending by use of rope and pitons. At first, we use a 50 foot face for demonstration. Often the men run down several times before we move to a steeper and longer rock face. I couldn't hold myself from laughing at one fellow who was about half way down and became scared stiff. His feet started to wobble and quiver and he looked just like a marionette on a string. So far, we have had no casualties, but there have been a few close calls. One fellow slipped away while I was untangling ropes. He had climbed up over a pinnacle and out of sight. I heard him shout, "How shall I get down?" We wasted a good hour climbing up to him and helping him down. Our program for Thursday is the most advanced techniques. Piton or "Tension Climbing" is the most difficult and the most thrilling part of rock climbing. You use Pitons when the going gets rough. Since each group spends only a week here, we try to make it as easy as possible. With no previous experience, you can't expect them to be expert rock climbers in a week. On Friday we have an all day trip up into the snow fields and on the small glacier in this range. I have looked a long time over these mountains in search of a rare flower, the Edelweiss. I have seen one that was "pressed" but have yet to find one myself.

(Author's Note: *The Edelweiss flower only grows at high altitudes among rocky limestone peaks. Swiss tradition states that whoever returns from battle with Edelweiss is a brave warrior who has conquered the enemy and the most dangerous peaks. German Wehrmacht troops wore this as their patch to identify them as elite mountain forces.)*

The night before last, I took my crude pole and line and headed for the rocky ledges across the pond. I had one fly of red and black. I saw one about 20 yards out that was at least 20-22". With the rig I had, I knew I could reach 10 yards and hope that he would meet me half way. I flipped it out several times slapping the water but old "Fatty" didn't even wiggle a fin. I whipped it again and still no result. I did not notice the strike from another fish. I battled with him for three or four minutes when some fellows came by to help me out. One climbed down to the edge of the water to scoop him out with his helmet. I had him played out but I was still cautious of one last break. The fellow almost had him in his helmet when flip!! And he broke off. Then, I looked under the rock which I was standing on and there he was! In I went after him. He weighed about two pounds and boy was he delicious with the characteristic pink meat of the better trout.

I have come to the end of the page and with my narrative up to date, I close.

Much Love,
Ted
Bob Hearn is in Linz Austria 100 miles from me. I hope to see him. He's in the 11th Armored Div.

(The first two pages of the letter are missing. Ted was on a weekend pass in Austria, staying with a local family.)

...answered yes when we didn't quite understand or laughed when we thought the occasion called for it. For breakfast the next morning we had a bowl of porridge and a plate of beans. Their national drink, tea, was to be had also. I gathered from them that the average length of service overseas was from 3 to 4 years and those that were in that group expected to be discharged in about a year.

We spent Sunday morning talking to an ex Russian POW. He was continually slapping our backs saying "Americans, Goot, Goot!!" He will be returning home as soon as transportation can be supplied. On our way back we stopped in Spittal and hung around the Kensington Canteen. Several Austrian boys hung around us asking questions about the war. Finally, we told one of them we intended to spend the night in Spittal and would they find us a place to sleep. He ran down the street and returned in five minutes. He said his parents were preparing for us. We went to their home a little after dark to avoid any suspicion of fraternization. I should judge that the lady of the house was about forty and very hospitable. We were shown to our rooms where we dropped our bags. Being unshaven and dirty, she suggested that we clean up a bit. Shortly we were in the bath tub and she brought us her husband's razor so we could shave. We talked some before going to bed. The lady told how terrible the bombing was and showed us pictures of her four brothers. Every one of them had been killed. One in Russia, two in France, and the other she didn't know where.

We returned to camp the following morning with one more hitch under our belts and some pleasant memories to talk over later on.

This week we have a full artillery battalion to instruct, which numbers around 350 to 400 men. We have been accustomed to handling 100 men so you can imagine our plight as instructors. Yesterday one of my men climbed several feet up a chimney. He accidentally kicked a stone out and it caught another fellow in the arm, severing blood vessels. Together another fellow and I put on a tourniquet (darned if I know how to spell it). We made a saddle using bowline knots around his waist and seat and roped him down. We belayed him down the 50 foot cliff and the medics took over from there.

Wednesday, five men, volunteers (the Song says you, you, and you) from the rock climbing were asked to put on a demonstration for Genls. Crittenger and Hayes. I was one of the lucky ones. It turned out to be one of the most enjoyable experiences I've had with Brass Hats. Crittenger after watching the demonstration asked if he could climb the rock and try a repel from the cliff.

10th Mountain trooper rappelling down a cliff
Denver Public Library, 10th Mtn. Division Photographic Collections

That started the whole works going. General Hayes was next followed by lesser ranking officers down to a Major. Every one of them scraped their knees and warmed their butts from the friction of the rope. I was more than pleased to shout instructions to them. I had to check myself several times from bursting out in laughter.

At last I am back in camp again having settled down to finish out the end of the week. You can see by my varied experiences that instructing rock climbing is bearing me good fortune.

Walter Murphy wrote me from Rattenberg, Austria, 100 miles away. I hope to see him this weekend.

How is the camping life this summer?

Hastily much love, Ted

Dear Mom and Dad,

This is it!! What a day. It has rained incessantly since early this morning. I have managed to keep dry by crawling into my sleeping bag, which is supported by at least a foot of spruce boughs.

There was an article in Stars and Stripes (our daily Army newspaper) which stated that the 10th Mtn. Division would likely be occupational forces in the Trieste sector. It hasn't been made official as yet. It would probably mean a longer stay over here, for us, but I am still pleased as it will mean the end of combat or a prolonged absence of it.

Yesterday Ed and I bummed a ride over to Austria. In a small town just across the border, there is a German SS warehouse. We toured through rooms full of overcoats, caps, old shoes, winter equipment, etc. Most of the serviceable material has been taken. I picked up a pack of insignias and some inner soles for my Italian mountain boots

If I receive a letter from Bob Hearn sometime this week I am going up to Linz next week-end with Ed. It has been nearly three years since I have seen Bob, almost unbelievable isn't it?

When we crossed the border, the change was very noticeable. The farmhouses and surrounding countryside show a distinct difference from Italy. Of course, the people give anyone in a military uniform the cold shoulder. It is mostly due to the fear and uncertainty of what a conquering force might do. We decided to get around our non-fraternization policy by asking a farmer for a drink of water. At first, he was suspicious of our request but was never the less obliging. Our conversation with him was brief but during that time he loosened up a bit. We saw quite a number of pretty blondes, but we restrained ourselves from making conversation. It was hard to do but the risk was too great.

Caught one fish the other day. It was a little bit smaller than the two pounder. He hit a spinner with a small frog hooked to the gang hook. Then we trolled for about a half hour and the rain came so we quit.

Every Saturday night the townsfolk in Fusine (village within the commune of Tarvisio) have a dance. It's one of those typical shin-digs where everyone, including the smallest baby, turns up. The orchestra consists of an accordion, a bass fiddle, and a trumpet. It was a real jam session as far as the people were concerned. During the intermission one cross-eyed and slightly drunken man appeared in the center of the room with a handful of knives. I learned later that he is a Fascist. His partner stood with his back to the door while the Fascist tossed the knives at his head and throat. Several Italian Carabineri finally put a stop to it. I guess he was shouting something which the people did not particularly like.

They ushered him out at gunpoint and then the music began as the party resumed a normal state once more.

Twenty-one today. Impossible!! As far as any different news or reactions, I have none, except according to law I am a man. I'm independent, so to speak, but still look to you for guidance in furthering my maturity. I believe that during my two years in the army I have gained invaluable experience, which ordinarily would have taken many years of civilian life. A solid foundation is under my belt and I am ready.

Will Barker wrote me a lengthy letter describing his latest expedition with Rev. Smith. They got lost!! Ha. Ha.

I've got to build a fire and dry my clothes for tomorrow. We start with a new group in rock climbing.
Love,
Ted

July 11, 1945
(Tarvisio)

Dear Mom and Dad,

Last weekend, Ed and I packed our bags and headed out to Austria with the intention of seeing Bob Hearn in Linz. It being a nice day, we strolled along the road, refreshing ourselves with the mountain air, looking over the various houses and sights. We crossed the border a little before noon. The change from Italy to Austria is extremely noticeable. The homes, people, and countryside appear mush cleaner as compared to the rundown condition of Italy. Places that were bombed in Italy still lie in heaps. The people are definitely lazy and lack initiative.

Our first acquaintance was with an elderly Austrian gentleman who rode along in a truck with us. He spoke broken English and a little Italian. Ed knows German very well so the three of us got along pretty well. His name was Fisher and he lived in Villach. It seems as though he was an infantry officer in the last war but was too old for this one. We told him about our mountain training. He became very interested when we mentioned skiing and more so when he found out we knew of Prager, Schneider, Pfifer and Matt, all of whom he met before the war. We continued on to Spittal where he got off and arrived at Lienz around 4:30 P.M. Lienz is not the same place as Linz and so I did not even get close to Bob Hearn. I thought that perhaps there had been a mistake in the spelling. We were very cordially invited to spend the night with the Sutherland Highlanders of the 69th Regiment. The Scotchmen have a very difficult dialect in their speech. We just...(Missing rest of letter)

14 July 1945 - The 10th is ordered back to the U.S. for further training in preparation for the invasion of Japan. The plans call for the division to attack the southernmost island of Kyushu on November 2, 1945.

14 July 1945

CITATION

THEODORE G. HOOPLE, 31302591, Private First Class, Infantry, 87th Mountain Infantry, United States Army. For heroic achievement in action on 16 April 1945, near Mt. Corce, Italy. While holding vital, newly won mountain positions in preparation for subsequent attacks, Private First Class HOOPLE, accompanied by a comrade, courageously made his way forward into deadly artillery fire to reach a position where adequate observation could be had of the enemy emplacements. Making his way forward during the most fierce artillery barrages, he utilized great courage and combat skill in maneuvering through the treacherously rugged area filled with bursting shells. Continuing onward, Private First Class HOOPLE was seriously wounded by an enemy shell burst and though suffering from the terrific pain, he heroically made his way back to his unit. His splendid actions, showing notable courage and a keen sense of duty, justly require the finest respect, confidence, and praise of all. Entered the military service from Belmont, Massachusetts.

BY COMMAND OF MAJOR GENERAL HAYS:

C. J. KNAPP
CWO   USA
Asst Adj Gen

July 19, 1945
(10th mountain Camp at Florence)

Dear Folks,

Drag out the extra blankets and have plenty of blueberry pie and ice cream ready. I'm coming home!!!

I can't tell you when but it will be soon. We will receive 30 days leave so that will give me plenty of time to do all the traveling and still have enough time to relax and enjoy myself.

*Ted receives the Bronze Star for his exceptional actions
on the battlefield above Tole*

I just received the Bronze Star, five more points closer to a discharge. As of May 12th, I had 50. Since then I picked up six more for being overseas.

The whole thing came very sudden. We were working on the rocks one morning when we were told to pack our bags and move out. We rode a train down to Florence where we are camped now with the whole division. Rumor has it that we go to a port further south and then sail out. I won't attempt to write you again.

Until I see you.

Love,
Ted
P.S. Sent a big box with war trophies in it.

2 August 1945 - The 87th and most of the remaining troops of the 85th and 86th sail from Naples, Italy on the Mt. Vernon. They arrive in Newport News, VA on August 11.

6 August 1945 - News is received that an atomic bomb has been dropped on Hiroshima.

15 August 1945 - Japan surrenders. Hundreds of 30-day furloughs are issued members of the 87th, including Ted.

THE HUPMOBILE

Upon returning to the United States on August 11, 1945, the members of the 10th Mountain Division were dispatched to Camp Carson, Colorado, to engage in the army's favorite pastime— administrative paperwork. Many of the victorious combat veterans were given their favorite duty—thirty-day furloughs. Ted happily packed his travel bag and started the three-day train ride east. Most likely he stopped in Cleveland to see the Rautenburg relatives and then went on to Syracuse to see the Hoople aunts and uncles and cousins. Here he formed a plan to travel to Cranberry Lake in the Adirondacks to visit more relatives at their summer cottages and then to head east to the camps in Maine, where his parents, Tot and Nelda, were directing the summer activities at Camps Medomak and Med-o-lark.

Somehow, he convinced his brother, Howard Jr., to loan him his sixteen- year-old 1929 Hupmobile roadster. It was a "rag top", two- passenger, with a rumble seat in the back. Howard didn't need the vehicle so much for his medical school classes, but it was essential for his social life. He would have to do without it for a while. After all, Ted just had to get to Maine to see their parents.

Another coup he accomplished was convincing his Aunt Ruth Pearsall Hoople to let her fourteen-year old son, Robin, accompany him on the road trip. Why not? Cousin Robin was out of school for the summer, probably mowing lawns and flirting with trouble in his abundant spare time. After a couple of days of "making the rounds" in Syracuse they struck off north for the Adirondacks and Cranberry Lake.

Ted's plan was coming together. There were just two more pieces to be put in place besides the obvious visit with the Rautenbergs and the Carvers. When they arrived and greetings and celebrations were over, Ted unveiled his plan. He had dreamed of this opportunity to fish his way across northern New York, Vermont, and New Hampshire his whole life. To do this, he would need to borrow some gear, of which there was plenty down in the boathouse. Also, he recruited another cousin, seventeen-year old, Gene Carver. The parents gave their consent and Gene eagerly packed his gear in five minutes.

The next morning, they left with Ted in the driver's seat—Gene up front, and Robin in the rumble seat—with some of the gear and a freshly put-up care package from Auntie Babe's kitchen. Their bags were stuffed neatly into the leather trunk strapped on top of the rear bumper. Their first stop was the village store to gas up and buy supplies to add to the sandwiches and boiled eggs Auntie Babe had made for them. A case of beer was added on top of Robin's cramped quarters in the rumble seat.

Off they went down route 3 towards the Saranac Lakes. Shortly, Ted pulled over and declared that his left arm wound was bothering him and Gene would have to drive. Apparently, the stick shift combined with the steering wheel was a strain that inhibited his right hand from handling the cold beer properly. Seventeen-year old Gene was more than thrilled to be the Hupmobile pilot while Robin took charge of dispensing the refreshments.

They rode along Route 3 eastward without a care in the world on a beautiful, warm and humid August afternoon. At dusk, they pulled over alongside a rock-strewn stream that dropped off into a dark, quiet pool. Out came the fly rod and Ted, in his travel clothes, waded directly but cautiously into the water, his eyes focused on the darkest part of the pool. There had to be a "Lunker" of a trout somewhere in there. The younger cousins watched silently as he repeatedly laid the Royal Coachman dry fly to the right of a large bolder and let it drift around and towards the back of the pool. Again and again, he performed the same ritual, each time softer, each time more subtly. The sky was darkening with clouds and the moment was filled with urgency. There was definitely electricity in the air. This one was the best presentation, as the fly slowly spun past an eddy and the leisurely current drifted it toward the rock ledge. "Wham", a savvy old brookie gave it his best lunge. "Whoosh"! Ted set the hook and the fight was on. Both cousins grabbed for the net as he gave the old native some line. He kept just enough tension to let the fish feel it was in control as it was expending all its adrenaline. He played him, back and forth across the pool, not too stiffly, not too forcefully, trying to ease him away from the deadfall of branches on the left bank—let him tire but don't let him go. After seven minutes of unpredictable leaps and deep runs on the taut line, the fish was spent. Gene netted the two-pound brookie as thunder echoed in the mountains above them.

They had to camp there that night because the inevitable arrived sooner than they wanted it to. Heavy thundershowers from the west were soon rolling upon them, and they retreated to the Hupmobile, quickly putting the convertible top back up.

Thankfully, there were still some sandwiches and beer for an evening snack. They slept that night, damp and cramped, sitting upright. It was not very comfortable, but a far cry from a muddy foxhole halfway around the world.

The next morning, they retrieved the fat eighteen-inch brookie that was tied to a stringer at the edge of the pool. Ted had wrapped it in grass and covered it with a flat rock, submerging it in the cold water to keep it fresh. Suspended on a thin maple sapling over the small morning campfire, the big brookie made a delicious breakfast along with the three hardboiled eggs that were left.

The thunderstorm of the night before had long since dissipated, leaving the air fresh and the sky a clear blue. They started off again—this time with 14-year old Robin gleefully at the wheel—heading east and then south as they approached Lake Champlain. They intended to cross into Vermont on the recently completed Crown Point bridges. Once in Vermont, they stopped to restock on bread, peanut butter, and beer. The homemade blueberry jam, supplied by Auntie Babe, would make the sandwiches that Ted had dreamed of since he had left home.

Driving through the Green Mountains of Vermont and on towards the harsh granite of New Hampshire's White Mountains, Ted was reminded of the Italian Apennines only a few months in his past. Traveling east or west in Northern New England avails no direct route. The push of the Appalachian Chain is north to south, allowing travel only through valleys and mountain gaps. This is good fortune for the traveling fisherman, as everywhere, mountain run offs gush out of these gaps into picturesque streams below in the green valleys. These physical barriers and long circuitous routes through the mountains are the foundation of the iconic reply to the famous question posed by many befuddled tourists in the area. The standard and mostly truthful reply is, "You can't get there from here".

They stopped at every inviting stream along the winding roads so that Ted could cast a fly of his choice across the rippling water of some suspected trout lair. This scene was repeated many times over the next two days with results that ranged from flat disappointment to unexpected joy. Such is the mantra of the Fly Fisherman.

At the top of New Hampshire, driving east on old Route 2, they passed the stoic, now abandoned mountain house that had belonged to the Brooklyn, New York Hooples, two generations before. It had served as a refreshing country home away from the heat and heaviness of New York City summers. Unfortunately, it required a long, difficult train ride to get there. Although it was perched majestically on a broad granite ledge with breath taking views, it is no wonder recent generations had been drawn to the lush forested shores of Cranberry Lake. Cranberry was only two and a half hours by automobile from the city of Syracuse and its University where many of the Hooples had settled after departing from Brooklyn.

On they drove, freewheeling masters of the road and mountains, feeling quite good about themselves. Finally crossing into Maine, they made their last stop for gas and non-alcoholic refreshments. Ted curiously purchased a copy of "Hollywood Stars" magazine. He took out the pocket knife he had received in the mail while he was on the front lines back in Italy. Carefully, he sliced away at a page and removed a two by three inch black and white of a young starlet without the caption. He slid it in his wallet and tossed the magazine back into the rumble seat for Robin to peruse.

Two hours later, just in time for the evening meal, they arrived at Camp Medomak. They approached the esteemed Director's cabin. Tot and Nelda were sitting in the old wicker chairs on the vine covered porch. They were anticipating a normal dinner in the camp's large dining hall, a short walk up the hill. As Ted and his cousins approached and were recognized, looks of disbelief and then relief were exchanged before everything turned into a joyful reunion of family. Parents and a son, who struggled for the past three years with thoughts that they may never see one another again, were reunited.

Once everyone calmed down, the questions started to fly, but the camp dinner bell had just rung. One more question from Mom, always her biggest concern, "What girl are you seeing these days? What is her name?" Ted pulled his wallet out of his back pocket with a mischievous grin, flipped it open and showed her the black and white of the Hollywood starlet. "Oh my, oh my, oh goodness!" was all she could say as they headed to the dining hall.

Author's Note: *This story was told to me by my second cousin, Robin Pearsall Hoople at the 1999 Hoople Reunion. He was sixty-eight at the time and recalled the trip with the glee of a fourteen-year old hanging out with his two older cousins on an adult road trip. We sat in the Medomak Cub barn with both end doors open to the afternoon breeze with sunlight streaming in. His enthusiasm and vigorous humor combined with his deep baritone laugh made me wish I could have recorded his version. Among his many talents, he was also a great story teller. I took some liberties where I felt the story needed filling in, using knowledge I that I gained first-hand, and making embellishments only if I imagined they could have really happened.*

October 8, 1945

Dear Mom and Dad

I have a few a few spare moments so I am trying my skill on a typewriter. The furlough situation is still up in the air as to when I will get it. Perhaps in a few days I will have a definite answer for you. Received your letter the other day and I am more than anxious to be on my way as military life has become a great bore. Bob Phillips and I have been cooking for the entire battalion and regiment during the last week. What a head ache it has been, since both of us have had no experience whatsoever. I tried to make cream sauce for the cauliflower for dinner the other day. Everything seemed to go wrong; the cheese did not melt, and the flour stuck to the bottom of the pan. That happened at 11:30. I had a half hour to try again but I was reluctant to make the attempt. Finally one of the old time cooks came in for a cup of coffee and I nabbed him for the job. I can boil water anyway!

We have attended every football game there has been in Colorado Springs. Last Saturday C.C. played Herington Air base from Kansas. I was surprised to see Walter McQuade's name in the lineup for the flyers. If you remember he was on the Colgate team in 42. He had a bad day Saturday. Mostly due to a very week line. Once or twice he broke through for substantial gains, but most of the time he was lucky to make the line of scrimmage. In the third quarter he started around the right side of the line and was creamed on the ground by at least four men; that finished him for the day. Herington lost 43-6. It was a very poor game from all angles. Next week New Mexico Uni. comes up to play C.C. It should be a better game as New Mexico is undefeated in three games. I do not need to mention Syracuse's record. I had expected a poor season but it appears to be miserable.

Howard writes that he had a great time at Cranberry Lake. I do not understand why he was concerned over his marks. He probably thought it was a big joke telling us how close to flunking out he was. The big goof nut always has a trick up his sweater. Being a junior in Med school at 22 is quite an achievement and a good break too. I suppose his little Bette is madly in love with him as indicated by his last letter. Have you met her? She is typically H.C. Jr. style. Very sweet, moderate dresser, and a rather pleasing personality, nice build and fair looking. I am afraid my tastes are for a little more glamour or umph as the bobbysockers call it. I love em all though and intend to play the field for quite some time to come.

I have since the war ended, had the feeling of an empty victory for us. I do not know just where to put my finger on it but things are not quite as I had expected. Perhaps I am all wet but that feeling still prevails.

Hoping to be with you soon.

With love, Ted

November 1st, 1945

Dear Mom & Dad:

   Need I tell you what a wonderful time I had with you these past 15 days? I wish to thank you for every moment of it.

   At approximately 11:45 P.M. on Oct. 28th the MP's asked for my papers. I showed them to one burly fellow and waited for his comment, which was no more than, "You aren't going to be there on time, are you?" and I replied, "I guess not." I was not awol until 12:00 PM. So at the time they stopped me, I was still within the bounds of my furlough. I had no further conversations the remainder of the trip.

   The train pulled into St. Louis about 2:00 PM, just as Nimitz was about to start on parade for the latest bond drive. I shouldered my duffle bag and went to the U.S.O. for a quick shower and shave in preparation for the hitch-hiking trip south. After a refreshing shower I caught a cab which took me to route 67, the main drag to Texas. I took several short hops before I got out of the suburban district. At that point a Missouri farmer hauled me approximately 60 miles and during that time he discussed the war in general—individual self-sacrifice, black market and various cases of immorality. He was a "chop-chop ear bender from way back in them their hills." He let me out at a roadside joint at which point I commenced my acquaintance with all the various persons which make up a hash house. It was 6:00 PM when I finished my dinner and prepared to hit the road again. This time I was picked up by a fellow who was hauling two cards from St. Louis to Fort Worth Texas. The only trouble with the set-up was that I couldn't go to sleep because it would tire the driver quickly. He knew the route well and every little chick in each roadside stand. Spent one night in Arkansas—Pocahontas. I believe, in a rooming house which he had frequented for several years while hauling between Texas and Missouri.

I arrived here on the 31st just 3 days late. So far nothing has been said and I doubt whether anything will be said in the future. I am connected with A.G.F. (Army Ground Forces) and I am working or will be working for a Captain as a clerk and secretary. Nuts!!! We take care of A.G.F. personnel and their complaints, which are numerous at this time. One other fellow is also working in the office. He is a nice fellow graduated from West Virginia and has taught match and has coached football, basketball and track at one of the local high schools in W. Virginia. This is the kind of set up which couldn't be bought for love or money a year ago. It calls for a S/Sgt and a T/4 rating.

I heard the points were dropped to 60 last night and the way people are talking I do not expect to be here over three or four weeks. They have been discharging one to two weeks ahead of schedule so perhaps the last trip home will come in the very near future.

Most everyone you meet here was in the infantry at one time and all of them waiting to go up for discharge in a few weeks. So far I have not found any with as many as I have. High man on the Totem Pole now.

There's a lovely park just outside the office and from the Capt.'s. chair I can see a golf course, swimming pool and several tennis courts. I'll have to take him on a game of golf when he gets back. Very warm weather.

Love,

Ted

November 16th, 1945

Dear Folks:

I was admitted to the hospital last week for a C.D.D. (Certified Disability Discharge) with the possibility of receiving a small pension. I have so far had all of my history taken care of but now I am awaiting a physical checkup. Following that I am to attend a CDD board meeting which meets once a week on Tuesdays. I hope to make next week's board but it looks rather doubtful. It's just a matter of weeks now and you can count on me for Christmas!

Every morning after details are taken care of we head out for the golf course which is open for hospital personnel. Clubs, balls and greens fees are free, so what more can a guy ask for. It's actually getting monotonous doing nothing from day to day waiting for a call for x-ray or blood tests, etc. If I make the board next week on Tuesday I will be discharged on Friday and home the following Monday.

I wonder if William has grown any? Is he still in the chewing stage? He's a pretty good dog don't you think?

Be on the lookout for white shirts. I realized how difficult they are to buy and also be on the lookout for suits and underwear. In fact keep a look out for anything that you think I might need.

It seems much longer than just 2 ¾ years since I went into the army. I'm glad it's under my belt and not in front of it. Yeah the next trip is one way and that day is not too far away.

Golf match in a few minutes. Have had terrific luck with my driving. But I have developed a bad hook with the irons.

You'll probably hear from me again—oh yes. I received the cap and insignia, thank you.

Love,

Ted

30 November 1945 - The 10th Mountain Division is inactivated

AFTERWORD

Ted returned to Camp Carson, Colorado on September 18th, three days AWOL from his thirty day leave. No punishment was levied and nothing was said as members of the 10th Mountain Division had earned special deference among the regular army "paper pushers" for their success and sacrifice overseas.

The 10th's casualties were among the highest of the war for a division: 978 KIA, 3,882 WIA, and 28 POW. On November 30, 1945, the 10th was deactivated.

Ted would be home for Christmas for the first time in three years. He reenrolled at Syracuse University, played on the varsity football team, married his Alpha Phi sweetheart, Martha Jean McKaig, and graduated in 1949.

Ted and Marty on top of Mount Katahdin, Maine, 1949

Ted and Marty had four children— Ruth Victoria, David Theodore, Peter Cranford, and Maren.

Ted joined his father in the ownership and running of the boys and girls camps, Medomak and Med-o-lark, in Maine, until 1964.

He eventually returned to Syracuse to serve as the Director of Annual Giving in the Development Office of the University until his untimely death in August of 1976.

The autopsy report stated that the cause of death was "Legionella pneumophila" or Legionnaire's disease. He was in Philadelphia the same week in June that there was a serious outbreak at an American Legion convention. He had stayed at a hotel across the street from the convention. Also, exposure to the smog from the supply train during winter training in the Pando valley caused chronic lung damage to many of the 10th Mountain troopers, including Ted. That, combined with his smoking habit, also picked up while at Camp Hale, made him a high risk candidate for the Legionnaire's strain of pneumonia. He passed away at the Waldo County General Hospital while on vacation in Maine seven years after his wife's death. To this day, I believe he died of a broken heart.

But, his charisma lives on. Cousin Gene Carver said of him in 2005, "Whenever he walked into a room, everyone would just light up".

Theodore Gordon Hoople, 1924-1976

BIBLIOGRAPHY

Burton, Hal. *The Ski Troops*. New York: Simon and Schuster, 1971.

Dusenbery, Harris, and Wilson P. Ware. *The North Apennines and Beyond with the 10th Mountain Division*. Portland, Oregon: Binford and Mort, 1998.

Earle, George F. *History of the 87th Mountain Infantry, Italy, 1945.*

Imbrie, John, *Chronology of the 10th Mountain Division in World War II, 6 Jan 1940- 30 November 1945, 2004.*

Feuer, A.B. *Packs On, Memoirs of the 10th Mountain Division in WWII*. Stackpole Books, 2004.

Jenkins, McKay. *The Last Ridge: The Epic Story of the U.S. Army's 10th Mountain Division and the assault on Hitler's Europe*. Random House, 2003.

Mathews, Tom. *Our Father's War: Growing up in the Shadow of the Greatest Generation*. Broadway Books, 2005.

Made in the USA
Middletown, DE
08 June 2023

32273236R00136